She Named Me Bruce:

A Daughter's Discovery of Her Parents' World War II Romance

For Jerry –
Happy reading!
Brucie

Bruce Anne Parcell Shook

Published by Little Lulu Publishing
24 Cape May Point
Greensboro, NC 27455

Printed in the United States of America

Library of Congress Control Number: 2017910999
Little Lulu Publishing, Greensboro, NC

ISBN: 978-0692919279

Dedicated to the memory of my parents,

Frances Parcell McNeely (1920-2008)

and

Bruce Fraley Parcell (1917-1944)

and to

my friend Janie Simon,

*whose surprising phone call set me on the path
that led to this book.*

INTRODUCTION

I am a child of World War II. I bear the name of a father whom I never knew. All my life I have heard fragments of stories about him and about my parents' brief married life. After my father's death in the war, my mother tucked away most of her wonderful and terrible memories and tried to start life anew. She had certain tidbits that she liked to talk about, but those revealed little about the deep love they shared and almost nothing about how it came to be.

When Mother died in 2008 at the age of 87, I inherited all the memorabilia of her life as it related to my father. This included hundreds of letters that they exchanged between 1939 and 1944, the year of his death and my birth. Dutifully, I brought them home and sorted them, as they were in disarray. Mother's went in one pile, my father's in another. Then I read them. They were interesting and emotionally difficult to read, but not compelling. Only when I decided to sort them by date, interfiling them so that their correspondence became a conversation, did the true story line become clear. And what a story it is! But I need to begin at the very beginning.

A NOTE TO THE READER

What you are about to read is the result of dozens, probably hundreds, of hours spent transcribing my parents' letters and researching their past from what meager resources I could find. One of the first difficulties I encountered was putting them in the correct order. Postmarks are often poorly stamped or smeared beyond recognition. In some cases there is a date with a month and year in the actual letter, but more often than not, you will find something like "Sunday nite." By using context plus calendars from the 1940s, I did my best to order them correctly.

Initially, I had planned only to write brief introductions to each section and let the letters speak for themselves. When my print-outs grew to fill two big fat notebooks, I knew I needed a different approach. No one was going to want to read all those letters. It became necessary to use excerpts and short quotes from the letters to tell the over-arching story. In some cases letters appear in their entirety; most have been pared down to communicate information important to the narrative. Some were not included at all.

Neither of my parents was a great stylist. Sentences can often be convoluted and hard to follow. Unless the meaning got completely lost in the forest of words, I left them as written. Occasionally I used editorial privilege to rearrange sentences so that they made more sense.

My father Bruce sometimes referred to my mother as Frances but mostly he used her college nickname, Lulu or Lu. In my narrative, I have used her given name Frances throughout, rather than switching back and forth. After they were married, she gave Bruce the nickname Pop or Poppy. I have no explanation as to why. She never told me about that. Ironically, our grandchildren call my husband Poppy, the name we taught them to use.

Finally, I must say a word about punctuation and spelling. Both Bruce and Frances made excessive use of dashes. In many places I have replaced those with commas to make the sentences flow more smoothly for modern readers. I have sometimes corrected their apostrophe usage for the same reason. Badly misspelled words, while infrequent, have also undergone correction. My goal in transcribing was to tell the story of my parents' relationship in as clear a way as possible while still being true to the words they wrote. When I began, I only knew a few small stories. As the letters provided me with more insights, a full-blown romance began to come into focus. But enough of this. It is time for you to read the story.

CAST OF CHARACTERS FROM THE LIVES OF FRANCES AND BRUCE

FRANCES:

Leila McNeely Lowrance and Jay Hepburn Lowrance: *Frances's parents*

Ruth Lowrance Rhyne: *Sister*

Wilson Lowrance, aka Skinny: *Brother*

Frances Lowrance, aka Frankie: *Wilson's wife*

Fred Lowrance : *Brother, killed in action, 1943*

Jo Ann and Shirley Rhyne: *Ruth's daughters*

Grandfather McNeely: *Frances's maternal grandfather*

J.B. Johnston: *Barium Springs Orphanage Superintendent*

Leila Johnston: *J.B. Johnston's daughter and Frances's best childhood friend*

Joe Johnston: *Leila's brother, killed in action, 1944*

Anne Branan Winslow: *College roommate and life-long best friend*

Dr. Jim Winslow: *Anne's husband*

Charlie Johnson: *Jim's best friend and Frances's one-time fiancé*

BRUCE

Katherine Fraley Parcell, aka Mama Kate and Tony Parcell: *Bruce's parents*

Blanche Parcell: *Oldest sister*

Katherine Parcell Graham: *Sister*

Nancy Parcell Aycock: *Sister*

Sarah Parcell Howard: *Sister*

Aunt Fanny White Moore: *Bruce's aunt, Mama Kate's sister*

Leonard Fort: *Friend of Bruce and Frances from Barium Springs. Killed in action, 1944.*

Harry Gillett: *Air Corps roommate in California*

Toni Gillett: *Harry's wife*

Sandy and Frances Johnston: *Air Corps friends*

Jim Ferguson: *Bruce's first commanding officer in the 405th Fighter Group*

Bob Delashaw: *Air Corps friend and commanding officer of the 405th after Ferguson*

Ralph Jenkins: *Air Corps friend who replaced Bruce as leader of the 510th Fighter Squadron*

IN THE BEGINNING : THE LOWRANCES

My maternal grandparents were natives of Iredell County, North Carolina. Jay Lowrance and Leila McNeely, known to her friends as Lee, were married in 1907 when he was 28 and she was just 21. He had attended Davidson College. He then became a teacher in a one room school house in an area of the county known as Coddle Creek. By 1912 they had two daughters, Ruth and Margaret. Sadly, Margaret contracted pneumonia and died on January 12, 1914. She was not yet two years old. On January 29, Jay and Leila moved with four-year old Ruth to Barium Springs, North Carolina, where Jay went to work for Barium Springs Orphans' Home. Enduring the death of a child, moving to a new place, and starting a new job were all life altering events. To have them all happen at once must have been a heavy burden for this young family.

Jay Hepburn Lowrance

Barium Springs took its name from the nearby natural mineral springs believed to have healing properties. Located just a few miles south of Statesville, North Carolina, it was at one time a health resort where people came to "take the waters." After a time, it fell out of favor, but in 1891 there was still a two- story wooden frame hotel there. The leaders of the Presbyterian Orphans' Home in nearby Charlotte decided to move several of the children from that establishment to the countryside of Barium Springs. These boys and girls took up residence at the hotel, but not for long. In December of 1891 the hotel burned to the ground. Fortunately there were no casualties.

Leila Frances Lowrance

Rebuilding began almost at once. Soon Barium Springs Orphans' Home was a thriving entity, as close to self-sufficient as a place could be. The property housed a dairy, a truck farm, an orchard, a laundry, a sewing room, a cannery, a print shop, an infirmary and a shoe repair shop, in addition to the dormitories that were segregated by age and sex. Those dormitories housed the children, with six to a room being average.

The children all worked and attended school as well. The youngest ones, ages ten and under, shelled peas and beans in season. Bigger boys planted corn, wheat, oats, and silage for the dairy. They put out fertilizer, and used mules to plow and harvest the crops. There were many animals to be fed. Hogs had to be killed, scraped, and butchered. One hundred cows had to be milked twice daily. Chickens were kept for their eggs and their meat; sheep were raised for mutton and wool. These sheep were also the "mowers" for the grassy areas of campus. On the truck farm, the boys planted and harvested all sorts of fruits and vegetables: beans, peas, turnips, eggplant, white potatoes, sweet potatoes, turnip greens, tomatoes, corn, peaches, apples, strawberries, pears, grapes, watermelons, and raspberries. There were pecan trees and wild blackberries in abundance. With everyone working together, the Barium boys managed to raise eighty-five percent of the food needed to feed the residents of the orphanage.

The Barium girls had jobs too. They took care of the youngest children, waited tables, cooked, washed dishes, did laundry, canned the bounty that came from the gardens, and sewed and repaired clothing. At the orphanage everyone worked.

The orphanage campus was split in two by Highway 21, which was not paved until 1923. In 1924 chain link fences were erected the entire length of the campus on both sides of the road. Two underpasses were built so that the children could cross underneath the road in safety.

When the Lowrance family arrived at the orphanage, Jay did a number of jobs. He was originally in charge of the dairy. The family lived on the first floor of a house called Round Knob. The second floor was home to a dozen boys ages thirteen to fifteen, and Leila became their house mother. After a year Jay was put in charge of purchasing for the orphanage. By 1917 he had the title of Assistant Superintendent. At times he also oversaw the maintenance of driveways and walks and for several years had charge of butchering the hogs and curing the hams. In addition, he drove children to Statesville to visit the dentist, the doctor, and the hospital. Trips to Statesville were also necessary to buy shoes, clothes for the high school boys, and other items that could not be produced at Barium. At times he delivered five-gallon blue glass jugs of Barium water to people in the surrounding area.

Round Knob, the first Lowrance house at Barium Springs

Leila may have been young, but she knew a thing or two about cooking and keeping house. On Saturday she would ask a Barium boy to kill a hen for the family's Sunday dinner. She knew how to do the job herself by wringing the chicken's neck, but the boys preferred to chop off its head. She would then plunge the bird into boiling water and give the boys the job of plucking off the feathers. Boys also helped her to churn butter. Later on, she would use Barium boys to help her haul rocks to line her flower beds. She also used these rocks to build an outdoor barbecue grill, a bird bath, a bench, a rock garden, and a legendary stone fireplace for the living room.

In June of 1916, my grandmother gave birth to her first son, William Wilson, later known as Skinny. Fred Jamison was born about two and a half years later in 1918, the year that saw the end of World War I, ironically labeled "the war to end all wars." Fred was named for my grandmother's brother Fred McNeely, who died young in an automobile accident near North Wilkesboro, North Carolina, in the early 1930s.

1920 in America was a landmark year. In January the Volstead Act became law, ushering in the great national experiment of Prohibition by outlawing the drinking of

Jay and Fred, "going milking"

11

Frances as a baby　　　*Frances, possibly age four or five*　　　*Frances, age unknown*

alcohol. Then on June 4, Congress ratified the nineteenth amendment to the Constitution, giving women the right to vote. Woodrow Wilson was president, but soon he would relinquish his office to Warren G. Harding. His was the first national election in which women could vote. All this was prologue to the flamboyant decade that was to become known as the Roaring Twenties. And on August 1, 1920, after a long and arduous labor, my grandmother gave birth to her fifth and last child, Leila Frances, my mother. Born in the back bedroom of Round Knob in Barium Springs, she would spend her childhood and youth at an orphanage where she was not an orphan.

Frances, as the baby of the family, was coddled and somewhat spoiled. Her mother could sew like a professional seamstress and made her many pretty clothes. She took dancing lessons and lived in an actual house, not a dormitory, so she felt like the perpetual outsider among the orphans with whom she went to school. Her saving grace was her close friendship with Leila Johnston, daughter of the superintendent of the orphanage, the much loved Joseph B. Johnston. Leila was a fast family friend until she contracted early-onset Alzheimer's disease at age forty-five and spent the rest of her days in a nursing home.

Leila Johnston and Frances,
sporting new swim suits

Through looking at the many old pictures that are part of our family heritage, I can see that Mother was a very pretty young woman. She had lustrous dark brown hair that she wore about shoulder length, a shapely figure, and terrific legs and ankles. She looked like dynamite in a bathing suit. Because her mother could sew, she learned to do so as well. Consequently she was always beautifully dressed. In the high school class prophecy, the prediction was that she would become a model.

It was pretty much Frances's destiny to become a home economics major. Her mother could not only sew, she could cook up a storm and always wanted the finest home furnishings she could afford. She favored antiques as furniture, so the Barium house was filled with many fine pieces. It apparently rubbed off on Frances, who inherited all of her mother's homemaking skills as well as an artistic talent.

Frances in college

When high school graduation neared, her mother decided that Frances was too young to go off to college. She was only seventeen, because at that time there was no twelfth grade in high school. Money was also a factor, since in 1937 the country was still in the depths of the Great Depression. Her two older brothers, Skinny and Fred, were going to be in college at the same time, so it was decided that Frances, much to her chagrin, would attend Mitchell College in Statesville and commute there to classes.

By sophomore year, she had convinced her parents that she could manage on her own at Queens College in Charlotte. In order to afford tuition, she landed a job in the college library. This eventually gave way to her working as a model for art classes at the college, thus fulfilling the class prophecy. Her major, of course, was home economics, there being no major offered in her preferred field of interior design. Her letters home while she was at Queens are full of information about her studies and her work, but especially about her clothes and her extracurricular activities. She was apparently active in a church, because she was often in charge of a devotional or other church related activity. So-

Frances modeling for an art class at Queens

rority life was very important, as were the many dates she had with a variety of boys. And there was hardly a letter that did not describe some article of clothing that she had worn to a party, needed to have sent from home, or wanted to sew with some material she had found at Belk's or Ivey's. She bought shoes for

$3.00 at one point, and loaned a fancy dress her mother had made to her best friend Anne.

While at Queens, Frances, who had never much liked her name, acquired a nickname that would stay with her for the rest of her life. The staff had placed name tags on the dorm room doors so the girls could find their assigned rooms. One girl came along and read "Leila Frances" as "Lulu Frances." Somehow the Lulu stuck and from then on she was most often known to her friends as Lulu or Lu. When comedy films emerged in the 1950s starring "Francis the Talking Mule," she was especially happy to be Lu.

Dressed for a dance in homemade formal gown

During her junior year at Queens, Frances, now generally called Lu by all her college friends, met Anne Branan from Thomson, Georgia. Thus began an amazing friendship that lasted until Frances's death. Anne was a fine arts major and gifted with an exuberant and adventuresome spirit. She led Frances into many exploits that her mother most definitely did not approve of. But they had wonderful times together, becoming part of a social whirl that included tennis, dancing, church and sorority activities, and dating. It was Anne who decided that they should go to summer school at Emory University in Atlanta. Anne's mother saw this as a golden opportunity for them to meet boys.

The only surviving snapshot of Frances and Charlie Johnson.

This plan succeeded dramatically. Anne met her future husband Jim Winslow and Frances became "pinned" to a young medical student named Charlie Johnson. *(Only in about 2006, when I read Mother's notes for the autobiography that she was composing as part of a writing class, did I learn of Charlie's existence.)* At one time Frances and Charlie had assumed that when Charlie entered his residency, they would be married. Part of a letter that Frances wrote to her parents from Emory in the summer of 1940 stated:

At home during college days

Riding Patsy, the family horse

I declare, so much happens in between times that I write you that I just can't start with any special thing. The dance was real nice and I had a marvelous time. For once in my life I did not get "stuck." Boys from other fraternities came over to the SAE house so I got to meet a lot outside of the 2 main fraternities. Everybody was especially nice. I had promised Bob I would teach him how to dance Sat. night but I never got back to his side on the floor and he told me today he got tired of waiting and went to bed.

Every one of the SAE's and Sigma Chi's are just as nice (perfect manners) as they can be. They treat Anne and I just like we are two little lost sheep in the wilderness. They couldn't be any sweeter than real brothers to us. I just wish you knew every one of them 'cause they are such fun and just the kind of boys anyone would be proud to be seen with.

Yes, Mother, there are some other girls here besides us. They are all from Scott though so Anne and I are quite individual. We are always friendly toward them and when we aren't doing anything we go to see them but for some reason or another they don't think so much of us.

You all just can't imagine what fun I am having. These two weeks have been chock full of good times.

Write soon and I will too. Lots of love to all,

Frances

(from letter #9)

THE PARCELLS: A BRIEF HISTORY

Meanwhile, as early as 1939, when Frances was nineteen, she had started to correspond with Bruce Parcell, whom she had known since childhood. Bruce had lived at Barium Springs Orphanage, as did two of his sisters, Nancy and Sarah, although they were not actually orphans.

Bruce came from a family of five children. He was the middle child and only boy. His mother, Laura Katherine Fraley of Cleveland, North Carolina, married Tony (sometimes spelled Tonie) Eunice Parcell in 1910. The newspaper account describes Katherine, later known to her family as Mama Kate, as "a popular and accomplished young lady of the Old North State." The young couple settled in Roanoke, Virginia.

Their daughter Blanche was born in 1911, followed by Katherine in 1913, Bruce in 1917, Nancy in 1922, and Sarah in 1924. When Sarah was two or three years old, Tony became ill with blood poisoning that resulted from an injury he received while working for the Coca Cola Company. He died soon thereafter. Kate, with five children to support and no real source of income, attempted to keep the children together by moving to the family home place in Cleveland. Finally she made the difficult decision to place the three youngest children at Barium Springs. When the children arrived at the orphanage on August 27, 1928, Bruce was eleven years old. The three siblings lived at Barium until they graduated from high school. Mama Kate would ride the bus from Cleveland to visit them and, when it was time to part,

Tony and Kate Parcell

Tony and Kate with daughters Blanche and Katherine

Bruce as a baby in Roanoke, Virginia

17

everyone would cry. The children would travel to Cleveland for a few weeks in the summer, but, according to Sarah, they became bored and were happy when it was time to return to Barium where they had friends and a swimming pool.

At the orphanage it was Bruce's job to herd the sheep. There were no sheep dogs, so the sheep herders were responsible for keeping up with the animals, chasing them when they went astray and trying to keep them in the correct spot where their main job was to "mow" the grass. Because the campus was divided by a highway, it was necessary to drive the sheep across the road from time to time. One day Bruce decided to have some fun with

Blanche, Bruce, and Katherine back row,
Sarah and Nancy, front row

this otherwise boring job. He and a friend stopped the cars coming in both directions and let one sheep cross the road. After a few minutes, they would allow another sheep across. This continued until a Greyhound bus came along. The driver, who was not fooled by the boys' delaying tactics, tolerated this for about five more sheep and then announced that he was driving on. As Bruce's bluff had finally been called, he allowed the rest of the sheep to cross all at once. This little story reflects much about Bruce's personality.

In a letter dated November 26, 1928, Bruce wrote the following to his "Granny" Fraley:

Dear Granny:--

How are you getting along. I am all right and I hope you are to..

Granny I have only time for a note but I thought I would write to you. I got your letter and was glad to hear from you.

Granny you ought to come up here. I work in the morn and go to school in the evening. There are just a few things that I don't like about Barium but I wont worry you with them. I have been getting along alright with the boys and I have a good many friends. Well, as it is time for supper I will close.

With Love,

Your Little Grandson Bruce.

Mama Kate must have saved this letter, along with his report cards from Barium, and at her death, Katherine or Blanche preserved them. Bruce did well in school. In seventh grade he took reading, spelling, writing, arithmetic, language, geography, history, Bible, and science. His teacher wrote that "Bruce is a fine boy—honest and straightforward. He has gotten on well in his studies and has made real progress during the year." His ninth grade teachers were also complimentary. Miss McDade wrote, "Studious and attentive. Never gets into mischief unless led. Seems to have ambition and high ideals. Gentlemanly." Another teacher's comments stated, "Bruce is the best student in his class. He is consistent in his study habits and has fine reasoning ability. He thinks his problems through and is independent in his thinking. He has good group spirit and a social disposition." In his senior year he made A's in all subjects but math. First term he received a B+, but raised it to an A in the second term.

Also in his senior year Bruce was the recipient of the Ace Medal, awarded by the orphanage's faculty and staff to the person considered to be the "best all around" student in his class.

Bruce at Barium Springs

Ace Medal

FRANCES AND BRUCE: THE EARLY YEARS

During his time as a Barium boy, Bruce became good friends with Frances's brother Skinny. He and other boys from the orphanage became frequent visitors in the Lowrance home. My grandmother cooked delicious meals for them and considered them her "sons." Frances was around as the kid sister. The boys all teased her and looked upon her with affection. Thus did Frances and Bruce grow up knowing one another, thinking of each other in some ways as brother and sister.

Bruce in his young adult years

In the autobiography that she created for her writing class, Mother wrote a bit about her relationship with Bruce during high school and college. She said that her brothers and her friend Leonard Fort, plus other Barium boys, brought their dates to the Lowrance home where the boys were always welcome. Bruce came as well but never with a date. If she went to Davidson College for an event with Leonard, Bruce would go along, but without a date. Once, Mother, my grandmother, Skinny, Leonard, and Bruce drove to Tampa, Florida, to visit Mother's sister Ruth. If the "fellows" were going out on the town, Leonard would make sure that Mother was included, and Bruce always went along on those occasions too. These little morsels of information say a lot about this so-called brother sister relationship.

Like many Barium students, Bruce was able to afford to attend Davidson College because of scholarships that he received through the Presbyterian Synod. The church took good care of the Barium graduates. In fact, all five of the Parcell children graduated from college. At Davidson Bruce majored in business. He also joined a fraternity, the Spanish Club, became the captain of the cross country track team, and was a Lieutenant in R.O.T.C.

According to letters to his sister Blanche, during his time in college, Bruce held down several jobs to help pay for his education. As a freshman he

Bruce as a high school senior

Left to right: Wilson (Skinny), Leonard Fort, Frances, Bruce, and an unknown man, maybe Frank Purdy

worked at cleaning out old buildings for thirty cents an hour. His next job was washing dishes. This enabled him to pay $6.00 towards college expenses. Second semester dues that year were $49.25. A summer job in 1936 took him to Fredericksburg, Virginia, where his Uncle Claude Parcell owned a company that supplied the eastern and southern parts of Virginia with Eskimo Pies on a stick.

Other observations in letters to Blanche reveal a little more about Bruce's thoughts during his college days. He made a C in Military Science, he said, because he had difficulty with map reading, but he was later able to raise this grade to A+. He wondered about the possibility of an appointment to West Point or the Naval Academy. In his junior year, 1936, he studied the new Social Security system in an accounting class and stated that he favored Franklin Delano Roosevelt for president in the election that year.

After graduation in 1938, Bruce decided to apply for a commission in the Army. He became an infantry officer, stationed at Fort Moultrie, South Carolina, just outside Charleston. He served

Running cross country at Davidson College

Picture is stamped June, 1939. Location is unknown, but probably it was taken at Fort Moultrie.

As an infantry officer at Fort Moultrie, S.C. Date is sometime in 1939.

there for a year, then returned to North Carolina as a member of the Army Reserve. It was from Fort Moultrie that he wrote Frances a letter, probably for the first time. It is dated January 28, 1939. She was a sophomore in college. At this point Bruce was not saving her letters, but he referred to them when he wrote to her.

Bruce and his sister Blanche continued to correspond. In June, 1939, he told her that he had applied for an appointment as a Flying Cadet in the Army Air Corps. By that time he was an unemployed college graduate living in Cleveland, North Carolina, probably at the home of his aunt and uncle, Fanny White and Neal Moore. He made it onto the Air Corps "eligible" list and was subject to call at any time. With no other viable job offers, he wrote to Blanche on October 25, 1939:

> As you surmised, I am still in Cleveland and still with nothing to do. I have written quite a few letters and have talked to one or two persons but it seems that I lack experience. I talked to one man in Charlotte who wanted me to sell Dictographs—on a commission basis—to offices, etc. I haven't written him, but I don't think I have the sales ability to get anywhere with it. Then I learned of an opening with the Mayo Corp. in the sales office in N.Y. Leonard *(Fort)* is working for them. It is an underwear co. They have 3 million-dollar plants in the South, and rate high. Then there is a prospect of a job in Winston with Prudential Ins. Co. So I am still plugging. I only hope something develops before Nov. 18, because if not I will accept the Air Corps appointment then, and I know Mother will have a fit.

Don't let this letter frighten you, and write again in a spare moment.

Love,

Bruce

(from letter #3)

He did decide to accept the appointment to the Air Corps. Even though in September of 1939, the Germans had invaded Poland and much of the world was plunging headlong into war, it still seemed his best alternative, given the struggling economy. He told Blanche, "I am still not worried about the future. What the heck! Life is so short and so uncertain anyway." This phrase was to be repeated in certain other letters as time went by.

These pictures from 1940 show Frances and Bruce as they looked when they were first getting to know each other better via the U.S. Postal Service.

In February of 1940 Bruce entered the Army Air Corps. He went to Tulsa, Oklahoma, and became a Flying Cadet in the Spartan School of Aeronautics. On March 11, 1940, he flew solo for the first time. From Tulsa he went to Randolph Field near San Antonio, Texas, for further training in the Air Corps' Primary Flying School. Randolph Field was considered to be the "West Point of the Air."

On March 3, 1940, before he flew solo, he had written to Frances, who was now a junior at Queens College.

Dear Lulu,

It seems like months since I left Charlotte. We haven't had time to think, and you know I have to have time for that. I start out at 6:30 AM and end up at 10:00 o'clock at night when lights are turned out—either going to classes or flying. Then besides studying, there are about 15 million other things that take up my time. So when Sat. afternoon comes around it is a pleasure to relax and write a letter.

How's school? Still making all A's? I'm carrying 4 hrs. of classes per day now. All new stuff mostly. Airplane engines, theory of flight, maps and math. It's the flying that's tough however. But I like it fine. Only hope I don't "wash-out", or be eliminated as about 40% of our class will be before it's over. You gotta be good to last in this game.

Lulu, rub a rabbit's foot for me and wish me luck about Tuesday or Wednesday, for I will probably get to "solo" then—if ever.

Toodle-lo,

Bruce

(from letter #4)

Bruce and a friend named Gil Erb on Monday, March 11, 1940, "solo day."

Hangar line, Randolph Field, Texas

Then, only a few weeks later, he wrote,

> Lulu, you are as bad as Mother. She is hoping I will be eliminated and sent home. But, it's not that bad. I like it swell, and still feel much safer in the air than on the ground. About the only way you can get hurt is to jump out, and even then you never go up without a parachute on, so even then you would be safe. *(from letter #5)*

After leaving Randolph Field, Bruce spent his final weeks of training at Kelly Field in the Air Corps Advanced Flying School. This air field was also in San Antonio. On October 4, 1940, he graduated as a full-fledged pilot, having earned his wings. Shortly thereafter he was assigned to the 79th Pursuit Squadron at Hamilton Field near Oakland, California. There he learned to fly a new Air Corps plane, a P-40.

In May of 1940 Winston Churchill became Prime Minister of Great Britain. The Germans invaded Belgium, Luxembourg, and the Netherlands. In spite of all this, Bruce wrote to Blanche from California that same month, saying, "Even if Hitler wins out, I see no reason for becoming involved."

He also confided to Blanche about a certain girl he had met in Texas, and about the political situation in the country. He sought Blanche's opinion about the war.

Bruce at Hamilton Field, California, preparing to go on maneuvers. He is proudly wearing his hard-earned wings.

...The little San Antonio Rose sent me a lovely big picture of herself, which doesn't bother me too much. She is very nice but...I don't know exactly what the score is, but for me it could not have been more than a summer romance. Maybe it was the uniform, or the Texas moon.

You know, the war situation becomes more serious every day. Even we are becoming concerned now. As a matter of fact, the higher-ups here are expecting and preparing for the worst. Our Group Commander has been in Washington and it has been relayed to us that his belief is that we will be in it within 2 or 3 months. This is disturbing news and especially so to us here, for we realize that the Army isn't prone to be as gullible as the general public. This hullabaloo you read and hear doesn't bother the boys so when they get serious about it I am inclined to feel that something goes on that we don't know about.

Still, what can we do now? We're actually in this war in every way except with men under arms and I don't see any possibility of stopping now. It's the same old story all over again. Wish you would express your opinion on the situation. Don't let all this worry you, for it doesn't me. I do know that this pursuit group is on the first priority list in every way, and that we need plenty of time before engaging anything or anybody in combat. I don't care to fight anyone's war but our own and this stuff about the English Channel being our first line of defense is a lot of baloney as far as I am concerned. We wouldn't stand a chance in Europe right now. But we can only sit quietly and let a bunch of fanatical politicians tell us what to do.

All this is confidential. Probably enough to hang me. But we all feel like history is about to repeat itself. What's your candid opinion? Do you have visions of Nazi troops goose stepping down 5th Ave.?

(from letter #12)

On June 9, 1940, Bruce received a letter from a crowd of friends who were gathered at Frances's home in Barium Springs. It illustrates how close knit this group of young people were. Here are excerpts from the letter, including comments from Frances and her family, plus a couple of other friends. Some of them address Bruce as Maude or Jay Maude. There is no indication of where this nickname came from.

Bruce (Maude), Sorry pal, but I am sorry you are not with us. You should fly over and see us. Wish you could join in on our semi-annual reunion. Love, Fred *(Frances's brother)*

Dear Uncle Bruce, I'm here now, but I won't be long! I've been good, but I won't be much longer! Please bring me an all-day sucker from Texas-or an aeroplane will do! Little Lulu *(Frances)*

Dear Jay Maude, In this cruel, busy, hurried, fast, and furious world one is compelled to think of the fact that life is too short and uncertain not to pause and relax under the spell of the finer things of life. However, we must admit that your presence is missed as much as a clock without a tick. We have just indulged in our usual excellent meal and now we are having our round table discussion. Wish you could have been with us. Leonard *(Fort)*

Hi Pal: I don't know what this is all about but I'm having a fine time. Kat and I are celebrating the turn of the century-or rather they are celebrating-Kat and I are watching. Got your epistle today and 'preciate it lots. No news since I wrote a week ago. Keep it in the air 'ol boy and you'll get there some of these days. Wish you could be up for this pow wow. Love to you and all the family. Skinny *(Frances's brother, aka Wilson)*

Dear Bruce: Maude I know you are busy and don't have much time and all that; but sometime within the next yr. or two if it doesn't push you too much, I would love to have an answer to that letter I wrote you some three or four months ago. I enjoyed your one letter so very very much. It was interesting and you know we all are interested in you and thereby interested in hearing from you. Glad you are doing so fine this far-just keep it up. We have missed you tonight but I think you will see we didn't forget you. Frank P. *(Frank Purdy)*

Dear Bruce, I hope you get as much pleasure reading these notes as we have in getting the gang together again. When you fly over for the week-end I will blow the horn for another home coming. Hoping you much success in your field, I am your friend. J.H. Lowrance *(Frances's father)*

Dear Bruce, They think this won't be complete unless I write a line. Did they tell you we were living down in the field now? The old crowd is here tonite .Wish you could be with us. Be good. We do miss you. Lots of love, Mrs. Lowrance *(Frances's mother)*

In June, 1940, Bruce wrote to Frances from Randolph Field in San Antonio. As in nearly all of his letters to her, he tried to minimize the seriousness of his situation.

> I suppose everyone is upset over the war. We aren't too concerned about it here, except that it has brought another Air Corps expansion, and this may mean that we will be kept here as instructors once we finish and can qualify for the task.

A P-40 At NIGHt. THIS IS ONE OF MY PRIZE PICTURES - TAKEN BY LIEUt. GROSS, A CLASSMAtE, DURING FILMING OF "I WANtED WINGS."

Bruce saved this picture of a P-40. On the back of the photo, he included a note.

Life is quite different here from what we went thru at Tulsa. I like it fine and am getting along fairly well, except at times when I get the blues and wonder just why and wherefore. I don't know, but there is a certain amount of mental strain that we live under, and no cracks either for it affects all of us at one time or another. They say no one goes thru here without undergoing a change. I only hope it's for the better.

Being a flying cadet must have its compensations, for we are getting in the movies. Last Thursday we had a holiday and spent it having moving pictures made of all the various activities here. I can understand why being an extra isn't so hot, for we hustled around all day, changing from one uniform to another and back again. The picture is being made for and by the Air Corps and I don't know what will be done with it. Maybe you'll see it someday. I doubt if we ever will.

Frances, it seems like a long time since I left home to come out here. What gets me is the fact that everyone at home, having become used to my being away, can't understand that I should feel that way. I even get a little homesick now and then. Can you imagine that? Anyhow, they just don't bother about me very much, nor write very often. Letters from home mean a lot to us, so write to me in a spare moment.

Yours, Bruce

(from letter #7)

The movie Bruce described was *I Wanted Wings*, starring Ray Milland, William Holden, Constance Moore, and Veronica Lake. It was filmed at Randolph Field in 1940 and used 1,050 cadets in its cast of thousands. A *New York Times* columnist wrote of the movie, "Paramount set out to exalt the spirit and efficiency of the program whereby hundreds of keen American youngsters are now being trained to fly—as military pilots, firstly, and as the nucleus of a future nation of winged men." It was *I Wanted Wings* that first publicized to the nation the Army Air Corps program for training airmen. The U.S. had not yet entered the war, but many saw it as inevitable, making the film a popular one. The screenwriter, Richard Maibaum, went on to greater fame as the adapter of twelve of Ian Fleming's James Bond novels for the silver screen.

William Holden and Constance Moore, co-stars of I Wanted Wings, *1940*

The correspondence between Bruce and Frances was not frequent in 1940 and early 1941. In a letter from Bruce in August, 1941, he sheepishly acknowledged that Frances had invited him to her college graduation in May but that he had never responded. Then on October 3, 1941, there was a letter from Frances, the first one he seems to have saved. At least it is the first one that survives. From that point on, the flow of letters picked up.

Frances's college graduation came and went, and she got a job teaching in a high school in McBee, South Carolina. McBee is a tiny town in Chesterfield County, which borders North Carolina. She taught home economics and biology to high school students who were fairly unruly. Her salary was $80 per month, $30 of which went to room and board. She was also paying $20 a month on a student loan. In addition to her teaching responsibilities, she coached girls' basketball, directed plays, and coordinated school banquets. She and three other teachers boarded with Mrs. Cain, a woman whose husband was a traveling pharmaceutical salesman.

These young women quickly learned that life in a small town meant that everyone knew your business whether you wanted them to or not. The town possessed only one telephone, with an extension line that enabled interested parties to listen in on everyone's phone conversations. Special delivery letters and telegrams were brought directly to the classroom. Junior Pigg, one of her more difficult students, worked for the telegraph office because he was a good runner and could deliver telegrams quickly. He made sure that her students

McBee High School where Frances taught during the 1941-42 school year.

always knew when she received one and who it was from. The students teased her endlessly about receiving letters and cables from Lieutenant "Parnell." She was also corresponding with Charlie, her serious boyfriend from Emory, during that year of teaching, but none of those letters survive.

In October Bruce and Frances began to speak of getting together at Barium Springs when Bruce would be in the area. He wrote to her from Rhode Island but did not explain exactly what he was doing there:

Hillsgrove, Rhode Island, Oct. 6, 1941

Dear Francis, *(sic)*

Tsk, tsk, what a very sarcastic young lady you turned out to be! While I am busy fighting to save Louisiana from the Indians and mosquitoes, you reprimand me for not answering your letter. Why, you should be patriotic enough to help keep up morale by writing and never expecting an answer. Now I've really stuck my neck out!

We spent the night in Charlotte on the way here, and Mother came over to see me. We flew over Cleveland the next morning, and I had told her to notify everyone that the third guy on the left in the second flight etc. would be the local yokel.

The dope is now that we go to Wilmington, NC on the 18th and then to Charlotte again on Nov. 15 to remain until the 30th. So I hope we can get together some weekend anyway. How about it? Do school teachers ever get to go home or do they have to deliver talks on British War Relief to the Women's Auxiliary on Saturday afternoon?

Anyhow, I will be back in Charlotte on Nov 15th and expect to get around to see everyone.

We are 6 miles from Providence which is a very nice town. However, for the past 2 days I have been slightly ill and haven't enjoyed seeing

31

the sights. Our maneuver here does not start until Wednesday, and I expect to be feeling better by then.

This place is a mad house right now. Guys screaming and running up and down. Radios going full blast, etc. Most distracting. So be sweet and write to me while I'm here. Be good to the kiddies.

Bruce

(letter #19)

Monday night (Nov. 10, postmark Nov. 11, 1941)

Dear Lulu,

We've just had a squadron meeting and it seems we're in for a bit more hard work from now on. The un-happy thought is that we are not free to make any plans, not knowing what will happen from one day to the next. And the time grows shorter and shorter and I'll be having to get used to California and trying to forget N.C. Or rather trying to reconcile myself to being there .Did you really try to believe that life is too short and uncertain, etc.? Wish I were convinced. But remind me to stop worrying, will you? After all you're coming out to see me in the summer and Blanche says she is coming out sometime.

Now, Lulu, I want you to let me know when you intend going home again, and you can call me up when you get to Charlotte at 3-8811. Then ask for me at the 79th Pursuit Squadron. Promise? I want to see you again before we leave. And let me know what you have planned for Thanksgiving and if you can go to the game.

I found McBee on the map today. Perhaps I can run down there some day if the war does not get too bad. I'd like to see your city. Do I have an invitation?

Be sweet,

Bruce

(from letter #22)

Frances quickly replied at some length. Harry Gillett, the Harry whom she mentions, was Bruce's roommate in California. It sounds as if she might have seen Bruce and Harry the previous weekend.

Wednesday (Nov. 12, postmark Nov. 13, 1941)

Dear Bruce,

Coming back to saucy pupils and lesson plans is not my idea of a way to recover from a grand week-end. I was much too far gone Sunday night to plan a single lesson for Monday so the dear children struggled through a pop quiz. While they struggled I nearly broke my neck at each passing plane to see you and Harry, but in vain. Was I disappointed! Tuesday found me lecturing so hard I didn't have a chance to glance towards the sky even.

I've just come in from a district teachers meeting in Columbia and I must say this is one time I'm glad to see McBee. We were unfortunate enough to hit a convoy and it takes forever to get through. And besides I was starving!

Is it too terrible for me to live from one week-end to the next? Maybe it's the thought of a holiday coming up that gives me this happy-don't care feeling. I'll settle down in earnest after Thanksgiving. Oh happy day, will it ever come!

Reminding you to stop worrying would be like telling a duck to stay out of water. Anyway if you stopped worrying Harry would lose his job of looking after you. I've come to the conclusion that teaching school and trying to live a normal life is hopeless. At least California is exciting. McBee has given itself up as a ghost town as far as actual living is concerned. It buzzes with curiosity though if that means anything. I'm glad you found the city on the map. Don't let the war interfere with your making a visit to this industrious town, please. We could shoot some dynamite if necessary. I'm all for it myself.

In fact after all these years you should guess that I'm ready willing and waiting to go and do anything--within a certain amount of reason. Seeing you on Thanksgiving sounds like fun to me, only I hope it won't be to say goodbye. Trinidad or California shouldn't call you this soon. After all what has Trinidad got that the United States hasn't!

We disband school Wed. for the Thanksgiving holidays, unless the maneuvers give us cause to declare a few extra days on our holidays. My plans now are to spend the night in Charlotte and go to Barium Thurs. morning. When I get to Charlotte my life is to be lived as it comes and not according to calendar and watch. Nothing would suit my plans better than to see Davidson redeem themselves.

Always, Lulu

(letter #23)

33

Here is Bruce's equally quick reply:

Friday night (November 14; postmark November 15, 1941, Charlotte)

Dear Lulu,

Tonight I feel very good. Perhaps your letter helped. Harry and I went up to the game and Barium won 26-0. I enjoyed it, and saw a lot of people whom I hadn't gotten to see before. Then we drove over to Cleveland for a while. On the way home, we ran out of gas and had to get a farmer to take us up to a filling station.

Lulu, you did sound kind of blue. You seem to think it isn't possible to live a normal life in McBee. Well, perhaps you're right, but neither is California a place for it. That is, it hasn't been for me in the past. It could be exciting, but you don't enjoy things by yourself. So I can assure you that it will be all you expect and more too, if you come out to see me next summer. You know, I haven't known whether you were serious about coming or not, but I know this. You had better be, because I expect it now. I can't think of anything I'd rather have happen than for you to visit me at Hamilton. So start saving your nickels. Your long letter surprised me, and I seem to have improved somewhat myself, but I'm all out of stationery now. So I'll have to wait until I see you to finish it, I suppose. Write to me before Wednesday will you?

Love,

Bruce

(from letter #25)

Plans for Thanksgiving were pretty much solidified by now, with both parties seeming eager to get together.

Monday (Nov. 17; postmark Nov. 18, 1941)

Dear Bruce,

Only twice more do I have to go to the little red school house and pound and pound to no avail. It does take so much will power for the kids (and me) to keep still when the "war" is so much more exciting. I believe my neck has stretched two inches this week just from straining to see the planes flying by. My basketball practice has been interrupted ever so often because some daring pilot swoops down with a few acrobatic dives. I'm always afraid he isn't going to get back up.

Your reputation is definitely established, as far as letter writing is concerned. Your letter yesterday was the best thing that's happened these last ten days. Wish that mood would strike you a little more often. Guess it's about time I gave you a medal for an A-1 letter writer!

I'm submerged in a stack of work a foot high. At least my conscience about my school work will be clear for the holidays. I don't even want to think about school when I go home.

As far as I know now, I'll get to Charlotte about 7 o'clock, that is, unless the army prevents, as it usually does. I'll try to call you when I get there if the Colonel doesn't have you under his wing.

Keep your chin up

Always, Lu

(from letter #26)

TURNING POINT:
NOVEMBER 19, 1941, AND AFTER

Although their early letters were at first tentative, then more chatty and friendly, there was an undertone in them that spoke of something more. Neither Bruce nor Frances seemed to be saying everything on their minds. They went from signing off with "As ever," "Be sweet," and "Keep your chin up," to "Always," and "Love." The letters became longer too.

Suddenly, on the Tuesday after Thanksgiving, November 25, 1941, there was a breathtaking change in tone and content. A very romantic, special delivery letter arrived in McBee from Charlotte, signed "With all my love, Bruce." What in the world had happened during that long holiday weekend that they had so breezily planned?

To piece together events, it helps to know that Thanksgiving fell on November 20. Frances had agreed to meet Bruce at the Charlotte bus station on November 19. The letters say that they stayed in Charlotte that evening and may have been at Barium Springs for the remainder of the holiday. In a later letter Frances mentioned that on Wednesday night, they sat up by the fire until 3 AM, talking into "the wee hours." On that day they somehow discovered that they were in love. Marvelously, hopelessly, head-over heels in love. They had known each other most of their lives. Frances had always thought that Bruce considered her the pesky little sister, good for picking on and teasing. To think that he might actually love her was in the category of a fairy tale. He apparently thought she was simply unattainable. Now they were at a crossroads. It was the worst timing imaginable. Shakespeare famously wrote, "The course of true love never did run smooth," and for these two star-crossed lovers, nothing could have been more accurate.

What is truly astonishing about this sudden discovery of love is that it is something my mother never shared with me at all. I sometimes used to ask her to tell me things about her early relationship with my father. All I ever got was the brother-sister routine, after which she would say that they started writing letters and "dating" and then decided they were in love. The reality as it unfolds in the letters that follow is far more romantic and fascinating than her abridged and evasive story.

Bruce was sent back to California immediately after Thanksgiving, and Frances went back to her teaching job. At this point letters flew back and forth almost daily. War was looming and the future was uncertain. What were they going to do? They were so young and so in love. Frances was twenty-one,

Bruce twenty-four. On some level they both knew this was all too good to be true. The letters alternated between giddy happiness and serious reflection about the future. Here, in part, is the first one.

Monday night (Nov. 24, postmark Nov. 25, 1941
Charlotte, special delivery)

Dearest Lulu,

How's my social outcast? If you have any trouble with the blue bloods, you tell me and I'll write the mayor, or better, drop a few bombs on the outskirts. Did you get some sleep? I did and felt guilty about it too.

Darling, why do I deserve to be so happy? I am, you know, or did I mention it before? Anyhow, I want to cheer you up, so smile pretty and don't worry like me. I've been thinking about you all day and it doesn't seem that you are so far away. I'm not unhappy so don't you be either. If you are, write me a letter and tell me what a cad I am and maybe you'll feel better.

I just got back from Cleveland--early too--10:00 o'clock. Jim Ferguson *(Bruce's commanding officer)* called me in and told me that I have a new job now--Squadron Engineering Officer. It's a big responsibility to keep our planes flying and it's kind of a compliment for me that he gave me the job. He mentioned our leaving and I groaned and he became inquisitive so I told him just a little bit about us, and that you were coming to see me in the summer. And he said that I should remember he had a spare room any time you came. Isn't that a swell kind of a guy to have for a boss?

Lu, I'm a liar--I am lonesome now--right this minute and I want so much to turn back the clock to last night *(Sunday)*--or better still turn it up 6 months. But I have something to live for now and life won't be the same dull existence it used to be. It hurts me to think that you are unhappy or lonesome, so promise me again to try not to be. But don't try to forget me, because I don't want to have trouble with you. And I have a little confession to make, too. I am a little bit jealous about another guy. Just a little bit, though, because I love you so. I've kind of been walking around on air all day, and I've had a swell time making plans for your summer. You see, I'm going to be firm with you again and I'll be that way until you smile at me and then I can't be firm any more. But I won't have to twist your arm, for my plans are just to try to make you happy and we are going to be, if I have to include the biggest spree we ever went on, on short notice.

Forgive me this short letter, but I'll improve with time and you will have to be patient with me. I've got so much to say, so many things to tell you.

With all my love,

Bruce

(from letter #27)

"Another guy" that Bruce might be a little jealous of was almost certainly Charlie Johnson, the Emory University medical student to whom Frances had been pinned (read "engaged") since the summer of 1940. She would find it very hard over the coming weeks to explain that relationship to Bruce. She was also now faced with having to tell Charlie about Bruce. But mostly the newly-in-love couple was concerned with dealing with their new-found feelings and their hopes for seeing each other in the summer. Here are Frances's first letters to Bruce after Thanksgiving.

Tuesday night (November 25; postmark November 30, 1944)

Dearest Bruce,

It is still so amazing that it seems strange to say dearest without having scruples about your detecting the meaning. Guess I'll have to break this indifferent air by saying that this is the most wonderful feeling I've ever had—in fact I don't believe I can ever say I'm unhappy again. Naturally this is one exception---when you'll be so very far away.

Haven't heard much about my late arrival but even so it matters not because I couldn't have had it otherwise. Hope you'll forgive me for being such dull company coming back Sunday night but for some odd reason I was concentrating fairly hard on keeping my eyes open and my mind off of good bye.

You know I did a very sensible thing yesterday. After trying so hard to keep awake and still make my lectures intelligent, I came home and slept until six-thirty. Then went to bed at ten. Guess that catches me up on sleep but it hasn't erased these perfect hours I've spent with you since Wednesday. Bruce you just can't know how happy I am—my one consolation now is that Saturday is only three days off.

Being so lonesome for you since Sunday has made me wonder how Harry can stay away from Toni so long. The army makes a lot of things possible though, doesn't it? Have you been flying this week? Every plane that passes nearly gives me heart failure. The kids are amazed that I let them look at the planes—if they only knew it was for a very selfish reason!

(from letter #30)

Wednesday night (Nov. 26; postmark Nov. 27, 1941)

Dearest Bruce,

Can this be me? I don't know what's happening but I have to write to settle my mind a little. Hope you don't mind my writing when I feel like it 'cause somehow it brings you a little nearer if I can write. Anyway I waited many years to be able to do this and not feel like I shouldn't have. You cad-you've really given me trouble and the best years of my life at that!

Darling--I'm full up to here with things to say but it just won't come out. All this that's happened since Wed. has made me afraid to breathe for fear it won't be true. Did you understand me to say that I love you? Remind me to tell you sometime-maybe on a spree.

I hate to bring up the subject but you said you would be very imprac-tical and see me before returning to Calif.—when are you leaving? Bruce, I've been trying so hard not to think about your leaving but it pops out when I forget my "Life is too short and uncertain" theory. Six months isn't long though I guess especially if I get such cheery letters as you've been writing. Would you mind giving me a few pointers?

The tanks passing just in front of the house are causing me to have the jitters. The soldiers seem so happy--I'm glad maneuvers are over. I'm most unhappy that they're over because it takes you away from me.

(from letter #31)

They really thought that they would be together again for a weekend before Bruce went back to California. As it turned out, they were not to see each other again for months; they would have to live for a while on the memory of those brief few blissful days at Thanksgiving. Over the next long ninety-eight days, seventy-eight letters were exchanged. They were filled with love and longing and a lot of ambivalence about what their future together would be. There was also a sense of wonder about it all. How could they have loved each other for so long and not have known it before now? It really cements that old cliché about absence making the heart grow fonder. The letters speak for themselves. In this one, written while he was still in Charlotte, Bruce mentioned marriage for the first time, although it is safe to assume that this was a major topic for discussion on that magical night when they discovered that they were in love.

Tuesday evening (Nov. 26 1941)

Hello little tough girl,

I miss you so much, Lu, already. But I've been a good
boy today, not grouchy or mean to anybody, and I didn't
get mad when someone appropriated my oxygen mask.
So, see what a good influence you are. Maybe I'll even reform alto-
gether someday. I know I will if you will get angry enough to tell me to.

Lu, all week thru Friday we're going to be flying early until late so I
won't say that I even have the slightest idea that I can get to McBee.
But if anything happens and a chance arises, I will surprise you .Nor
can I plan anything for Saturday. I know this, however. I refuse to go to
California without seeing you again-and that is far from being practical.
In fact it's mutiny.

A boy in the squadron went to Florida over our holiday and got married. Perhaps we should have gone to Tampa. Anyway we all had a
piece of his wedding cake today. I'm not just saying that darling, and
there's nothing in the world that I want more than for us to be married.
If I had not felt that way I would not have told you that I love you. It was
so hard to tell you though, because I didn't want to tell you that and
then ask you to wait for me. I don't know, Lu, perhaps I was afraid you
wouldn't want to wait. Why, a week ago neither of us knew how the
other felt. It's all so strange, and I've been happier than at any other
time in my life. Being with you seemed to have been meant to be that
way. I've been so blind all these years. Perhaps I can make up for it
some way, some day.

(from letter #28)

A recurring theme was how little they knew each other, in spite of having
known each other for so long. Bruce wrote:

Isn't it strange that we know each other so well and yet really don't at
all? Now I'm afraid for you to get to know me real well because you
might not like me, after that. Here I go—off again—you just ignore
some of the things I say, for perhaps I'm not responsible. It's a lot easier
for me to talk to you than to write. I've got to see you again, Lu.

(from letter #29)

And Frances soon replied:

I've wanted to write you five or six times a day but there seems to be
a little bit of practical (again) Frances that is still a little bit afraid that

something is going to happen. Does that make sense? Doubt it—but I'll have to be very frank with you because for some reason I can't be otherwise. You've made me so happy and yet, as you say, we seem to know each other and yet not at all. Bruce—no matter what I don't know about you—the person I know now would make up for anything else—even moodiness. Incidentally, I've been feeling the same way—afraid that you might not like me as well. I suppose we're both going to have to have an understanding and straighten out all the fears so we can talk and write without the other being doubtful about the meaning. Guess I'm getting complicated too and besides that I'm working myself into a very blue mood.

Bruce, as soon as you know when you all are leaving, let me know—so I will have a little time to get prepared—I really don't like that type of surprise. I've been having bad dreams about you going to Calif. without my seeing you again.

(from letter #32)

These next letters were fairly typical of the sorts of conversation that went on and on and on. Trying to carry on a long distance romance after having only a long weekend to kindle it was proving difficult.

Sunday night (Nov. 30, 1941)

Dearest Lu,

You can't imagine how bad I feel about what has happened. Twenty minutes after talking to you, I found out we really were leaving at 1:00 *(for California)*. All the things I said about seeing you before I left were just wishful thinking, and I had no right to say them. Darling, will you forgive me? My plans make no difference to Uncle Sam and I should realize that by now.

We spent last night in Shreveport, La. But I was unable to write to you. It's the first night I've missed except Fri. and I was expecting to see you Sat. Well, we got to Dallas at noon today. When we took off again, one of the fellows had some trouble with his landing gear. His wheels would not retract and neither was he sure they would go down properly. So he dropped his auxiliary fuel tank in a lake near the field and landed again. This tank hangs underneath the plane and can be released in emergency. He landed ok and Jim sent me back to stay with him until his plane is fixed. We expect to leave sometime tomorrow. That is what has happened to me.

I hope you got my wire before 2:00 o'clock, for I didn't want you to be waiting for my call and be disappointed too much. Lu, I was so upset that I couldn't talk to you on the phone. Don't think too badly of me. After all, I didn't say good bye and perhaps that is good too. I don't want to ever say that for long.

Lu, your letter worried me a little. You said something, however, that I appreciated more than you can realize. About what you thought of me—But darling it wasn't necessary about the past you spoke of. For there aren't any deep dark secrets in my life. What did I say to make you feel that something was wrong? I've never had any secrets from you, and I'll always try to be truthful with you. You seemed worried about me. You said you were afraid something was going to happen. What was it? I don't know of anything worse that could have happened to me than leaving without seeing you. I thought about you all the way here and woke up this morning thinking of you. Lu, I love you. If I've said something to make you feel like your letter sounded—it is just because I realize that my life doesn't belong to me but to Uncle Sam. That is what makes it so difficult. I have been optimistic and will keep on being so about us. The thought of seeing you and being with you again in the summer is my one consolation at present.

Please write, Lu and I'll get your letters at Hamilton Field. They mean so much now that I'm going to be 3000 miles away. Promise.

About not knowing what we mean in our letters, what is it, Lu? I don't want you to feel that way. If we don't know each other, it's only because we haven't had the chance. And I long for that chance, Lu. But please tell me what you feel, always. I don't deserve having you love me, Lu, but I want it so very much. Please don't forget that. Promise.

I'll write every nite and let you know how I am. Right now I am very very unhappy, and I miss you so.

With all my love,

Bruce

(from letter #33)

Sunday evening (November 30, postmark Dec. 1, 1941)

My dearest,

It seems weeks since you called me and it has been true eternity since the perfect Thanksgiving weekend. Sometimes I convince myself that six months is really just a short while considering all I have to do between now and then. Makes me shudder to think about it. Although I'm definitely not coming back to McBee next year. I would hate to be fired for not doing my work—or for keeping late hours at that! You're a terrible influence but somehow I'm crazy about the way you seem to be running my life. One thing definite—you can't give me trouble while you're so far away except make me think more about you when I should have my mind on something an inch nearer home, like scolding Junior Pigg. I know he's happy; I haven't even bothered to give him a second thought these days.

My students really are wondering about the change in me though—usually I'm pretty grouchy when they get noisy or don't know their lessons but believe it or not I've worn a perpetual smile all week. I did fuss one day, when I was in the midst of a lecture a dozen or more planes swooped down on McBee and played around for the longest time and no amount of talking would bring attention to me. The air force is certainly going to wreck the stability of all these little country schools, to say nothing of the nerves of the teachers, especially when the teacher wants to see what's happening and has to control her curiosity with indifference.

(from letter #36)

Tuesday Night (Dec. 2; postmark Dec. 3, 1941 Bakersfield, CA)

Hello darling,

Darling, someday you're going to get suspicious and wonder what in —--- is wrong with me and I'll say it's a lie because it wouldn't be practical to love someone so very much and be unhappy because of it. If I do, it won't be true, for it isn't a lie and I'm not practical about some things in spite of what you think. Is it practical to think about one thing so much? Or wish for one thing so much? Well, then my campaign must be successful. Yet, I know what you must be thinking, Lu. Do you still think I'm being too practical about us? I'd really like to know, but perhaps you know that I love you too much to ruin our happiness. At least that's what I feel would be involved and I can't seem to convince myself any other way. Am I talking in riddles again? I'm just trying to convince you that I love you and want you but that it wouldn't be fair to ask you to marry me now. Darling, maybe it doesn't make sense, but it's true. Please tell me what you are thinking as you read this. Besides promising me not to be unhappy, you made another promise that I haven't forgotten. I can't expect you to even want to keep it, because it's so unfair even knowing an aviator in Uncle Sam's Army much less having one run away on a minute's notice. Lu, I shouldn't have said all this because I do want you to wait for me and I seem to be trying to convince you not to. Darling, perhaps I'm afraid, too—that something will happen—that this won't be true. Is that what you were afraid of? Please tell me.

(from letter #37)

This letter was especially romantic and explained some things about Bruce's feelings.

Wednesday night (Dec. 3, 1941, postmark Dec. 4)

Dearest Lu,

I wanted you to know I got here *(to Hamilton Field in California)* safely—hence the telegram. It was a swell trip—as far as airplane trips go—but I dreaded it so. Still 3000 miles isn't far away with a P-40. Only about 12 hours flying time. And I will be back, Lu, I promise you. I won't know when until the last minute probably, but will let you know. I only hope it's on a weekend so you can come up, for I don't see how I could get to McBee from Charlotte. And I've got to see you, Lu. There was so much I left unsaid and so much to tell you that I can't seem to express in writing.

There is a full moon tonight. Lu, if you were only here now. I'm so happy now. Can you understand that? If you knew how things were before going home, you would. I love you darling, and that makes so much difference—now that we both know. Your letter written Sat. night was waiting for me and that made me happy too.

Lu, it was sweet of you to say what you did in your postscript. I won't be worried. I have so much to be thankful for that I shouldn't worry about anything anymore. For example the 20th Pursuit Group is going to stay in the USA for the present at any rate. That has kept me worried a lot, for leaving would mean being away too long to hope that you would wait for me to come back. Some of the new boys in the Group are being transferred out to go on Foreign Service but I will be at Hamilton Field, waiting for summer to come. Lu, I really was disappointed when you didn't come out last summer. And here is a little secret of mine. I wanted to see you because I wanted to have happen just what has happened. I hoped so much that it would but didn't think that it would. What about me, anyway? Lu, you said that you wanted us to be able to speak freely in our letters so that's what I'm doing. There are a lot of things that I'd rather tell you than write, but that is too long to wait. I wonder why I never kissed you before, for I have often wanted to. Lu, I've admired you for such a long time. To me you have always been the nicest girl I've ever known. Perhaps I never thought much about it years ago but while we were in college I felt that way. It is hard to explain because I don't understand myself. Perhaps we saw so much of each other that we developed a brother-sister friendship. Darling, I did tell Harry once that there was a girl in NC who I would marry if she would have me. I reminded him about it after that night and he remembered finally. But I always had the feeling that you could never be interested in me. Perhaps that is why I was so shy. And I never knew any different until that Wednesday night in Charlotte. It is strange, isn't it?

To feel that you love me and miss me is still hard to comprehend. And the way I feel now should be new to me but it isn't. It's just as if we knew all along. It would have meant so much to me to have had your love before now. Especially this past year when I was so lonesome. Perhaps I know what you meant about wasting the best years of your life. But that isn't true, for we have so much happiness to look forward to. Lu, I know we do and I want more than anything to contribute to your happiness. I want to be part of you. It's selfish I know, but I want you to miss me. I'd be very unhappy if I thought you didn't. And don't you worry about me either. I'm so very sure about loving you—or else I wouldn't be writing you like this. I know that it is my problem now to work out our future. Darling, you haven't said yet that you will marry me. I know that I haven't actually asked you, because I couldn't ask you to obligate yourself to me and then wait and wait. Please understand that that was the only reason I didn't ask you. And Lu, I'm not asking you now. I don't want you to say yes now for things are too uncertain. I just want you to know for sure how I feel about you. And now I haven't any secrets at all any more.

(from letter #41)

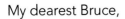

Home—Saturday (Dec. 6; postmark Dec. 7, 1941, 7 AM)

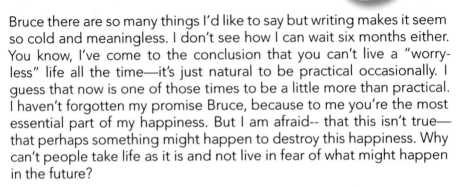

My dearest Bruce,

Bruce there are so many things I'd like to say but writing makes it seem so cold and meaningless. I don't see how I can wait six months either. You know, I've come to the conclusion that you can't live a "worry-less" life all the time—it's just natural to be practical occasionally. I guess that now is one of those times to be a little more than practical. I haven't forgotten my promise Bruce, because to me you're the most essential part of my happiness. But I am afraid-- that this isn't true— that perhaps something might happen to destroy this happiness. Why can't people take life as it is and not live in fear of what might happen in the future?

(from letter #42)

On the eve of the Pearl Harbor bombings, Bruce was thinking about their future again.

Saturday night (Sat. was Dec. 6; postmark Dec. 8, 1941)

Hello darling,

It is Saturday and instead of a week it seems like years since I left Carolina. And I've only received two letters from a certain party who has given me so much trouble because I did not write to her. Did you get my letters? Thursday night I didn't write because I was disappointed when I got no letter from you. And last night I was a very bad boy. My old roommate from flying school days came to Hamilton, enroute to parts unknown and I had to show him the town. We got home late—too late for me to write a letter. And I had to be at work at 8:00 AM this morning.

Lu, to bring up another subject that has been on my mind—and something I've worried so about, because I was afraid you would not understand. I'm speaking about our future. I think in my last letter I just about told you everything I have felt. Now I want your reaction. You must open up and tell me how you feel about it. You are unfortunate, Lu, to have me. But don't ever stop or you'll really have trouble. I might kill myself on your door step or some such thing. You don't know what a desperate soul I can be.

Seriously now, Lu, I wish you could know what a serious situation everything is in these days. I suppose there are some things much bigger than me, or my personal feelings and desires. I don't like to frighten you and I won't but I do want you to know something of where I stand. I told you in the last letter that we were remaining in the U.S.A. Well, that is true and I expect to be here next summer to see you. But the world situation is worse now than ever before—as far as we are concerned, and I supposed nothing is too certain. Lu, if I expected to be sent on Foreign Service I'd certainly tell you, so don't worry about that. Still, we have several fellows here just recently married who are being sent without their wives. Lu, I don't really know how I feel about that end of it. I just know that I have you and I believe that the war wouldn't stop me from wanting you to marry me. I don't know that I would expect you to want that –if I did have to leave. But Lu you would have to love me so very much to marry me. That is what frightens me. It's not fair for either of us to be in love at a time like this, but it is so much harder for you than me. I've been afraid, too, that you would not wait for me. Darling, I love you so much. And although I may be selfish, I don't want to ruin your life. The possibility of war is something we both must face and make a decision on. But I still feel that my other problem is mine and that I must work it out myself. Lu, you've got to tell me how you feel about all this. You haven't yet, you know. Darling, I can't ask you to marry me until I know that—or at least feel that—it would work out and I could make you happy and provide for you. It is unfair Lu—so unfair to you. If we could only be together. Like you, I have only the summer to look forward to. About a spree? Why, haven't I told you? Our summer is going to be just one big spree. I want you to enjoy it more than anything else in your whole life. I'm going to make you love me so much that you'll never never forget me. I mean it—Lu--I can't lose you now—regardless of wars and insignificant things like that.

(from letter #44)

It is impossible to determine just when this next letter was written. Often the postmarks on the envelopes were poorly stamped or smudged beyond recognition. It must have been written shortly before Frances knew of the Pearl Harbor bombing. It clearly was a Sunday, since she was preparing lesson plans for the next day. Given the six hour time difference between North Carolina and Hawaii, perhaps news of the Japanese surprise attack had not yet reached her when she wrote the letter.

Sunday night (postmark unreadable)

My dearest Bruce-

How can a person expect to do good work when there is something so much more pleasant to do –like reading your letter over and over. Bruce this last one was a masterpiece—you shall have your reward too just as soon as I have time to catch my breath! I've been trying for three hours to work out a simple chart of the circulatory system to show my students tomorrow and you're all mixed up with it. I'll probably spiel forth the contents of your letter instead of the biological facts.

I've just been listening to the news reports about the out-break in Japan and Manila and I can't help but wonder when things will start popping over here. You said you were stationed at Hamilton—does that still hold good? I don't know what I would do if you were transferred to Foreign Service. That's a gruesome thought but I'm beginning to learn to face facts—and I don't want such a thing to slip up with only an hour and a half notice!

Talking about secrets—you just don't know how very much I wanted to go to Calif. last summer. I thought—and hoped that I might at least settle my mind one way or the other by going—meaning that I might find out definitely that I was only a "kid sister" and would never be anything more or else gain a little encouragement. You know you never gave me much –or if you did you smoothed it over with something near sarcasm. That's what used to make me so mad. I could never discover exactly where I stood, if at all! Perhaps I was a little different myself but only because I didn't want you to know that I liked you so much.

If my missing you will keep you from being unhappy then you should be the happiest—surely six months won't be as long as these two weeks! Bruce I love you—I can't express on paper the way I do feel so you'll just have to read between the lines a little.

Always,

Lu

(from letter #43)

WAR AS EXPERIENCED STATESIDE

On the morning of December 7, 1941, Japan launched a surprise attack on the U.S. naval base in Pearl Harbor, Hawaii. Over twenty-four hundred Americans died in the carnage, and damage to the U.S. naval vessels in the harbor was immense. Bruce wrote the following letter on the evening after the attack on Pearl Harbor. Any doubts about the U.S. entering the war ended abruptly on that day. On December 8 President Franklin Roosevelt declared war on Japan. Shortly thereafter Germany and Italy declared war on the United States. The ground had now shifted beneath them and the future was more uncertain than ever.

Sunday nite (Dec. 7; postmark Dec. 8, 1941, 9 AM)

My darling,

There isn't much to say. You know as much as I—from the radio—Please, Lu, don't worry about me now. I expect still to stay here. This is something bigger than you or I. Just remember that I'll love you always. I'll write as often as possible and don't worry if I don't tell you much of what is happening.

I must get some sleep now for I'm very tired, and must be up early.

Lu, please keep writing to me. Write to Hamilton Field-79th Squadron.

I love you, darling,

Bruce

(from letter #45)

Monday evening (Dec. 8; postmark Dec.9, 1941)

My dearest Bruce,

These entire things that are happening seem just like the storybooks—I can't realize that we've actually declared war. My classes today have been nothing but war talk—the children ask so many questions and expect a most intelligent answer from the teacher. I'm afraid I'm almost as ignorant as they. Since I've been receiving so many letters from you the kids have been teasing me about "Lieut. Parnell." Today they really had your interest at heart. They were most concerned about your going to war. I'm not even thinking that. This living day by day is a full time job now. Reading about how pretty Calif. is now makes me envious. It is icy here and although it is invigorating, I've rather taken a sudden fancy to the sunny plains of the west.

Mary B. *(Frances's roommate)* has had me rehearsing all afternoon for our Christmas pageant. I'm representing Peace, but from the looks of things I'm a lost cause. It seems I do get myself into more unnecessary trouble. There are about twelve children that are supposed to be my charges and with their help I'm sure we'll cause an upset in the middle of a most sacred scene, but when I have to laugh I must—the children seem to be the same way!

I'm just rambling on here and all the while I'm so afraid of what is going to happen to us now that war is actually here. Darling, you will let me know if you're going to be transferred, won't you? Bruce, no matter what happens now or ever—I'll wait for you. It couldn't be any other way because you see I've waited so long for the inevitable to happen and now that it has, nothing could make me give it up, unless you wished it so. Sometimes I think if only I could see you for just a few minutes each day that I could live the day in complete happiness. Bruce, we do have a lot of happiness to look forward to and I'm trying to develop a little patience, because, now especially, I'm afraid that's what it is going to take.

To think that you love me is still quite unbelievable and as much as I'd like for everyone to know, I can't seem to tell a soul. Perhaps I'm still afraid it might be a dream. Hope I never wake up if it is.

Bruce-you're so good to put up with all my troubles when you have so many now yourself. I miss you so very much—and I love you—with all my heart.

Lu

(from letter #46)

It must have been frustrating for Bruce not to be able to be more forthcoming about what was going on in the wake of the bombing of Pearl Harbor. He always made the situation sound far better than it actually was.

Tuesday night (Dec. 9, 1941, postmark Dec. 10)

Dearest Lu,

The short note I wrote Sunday night *(December 7)* may have upset you. Sunday was a hectic day for all of us, and when I tried to write I was completely exhausted.
As you can imagine, starting to operate under war time conditions involves a lot of work.

I wish I could tell you exactly what is happening and what we are do-ing but you can understand that it is impossible to write about these things, even to those we love. Lu, I can tell you this—my plans for the future are the same, at the present time. With a war going on there is no way of telling what the future holds but then one can be optimistic. I still hope to see you next summer, but that may be being too opti-mistic.

Lu, I am mixing up my thoughts here too. Everything seems to pop into my mind at once. I want to tell you so much. At present, we are living under conditions much better than any encountered on maneu-vers, and as for our operations, don't worry about that. That is about all I can say here. You have seen a lot of stuff in the papers, part of which is true, a great deal of which is war hysteria. I sincerely mean that darling, and you must believe me. Actually I feel better right now than I have for some time. Now we know there is a job for all of us to do. There is an end to a lot of uncertainty that has kept everyone on edge. We didn't ask for this and we didn't start it. Now there is only one thing ahead and that is to get it over with as soon as possible. Everyone feels that way, and personally I am more concerned about you and the family at home than myself. We have a lot of confidence and faith in ourselves—maybe it is conceit—and the sooner we can end this the better. But there isn't anything I can say to keep you from worrying, I know. It is certainly all the world to me to know that there is someone who is thinking of me. Lu you mustn't worry too much. It is so needless, and I will be worried about you if I think you are too unhappy about this.

Smile pretty, Lu, and keep your chin up. This isn't something we both can't take.

With all my love,

Bruce

(from letter #47)

Frances tried to get her mind around how war was going to affect this fledgling relationship. She talked of "secrets" in her life, which surely meant Charlie.

Wednesday (Dec. 10; postmark Dec. 11, 1941)

My dearest,

Bruce, I realize and believe as you that at a time like this we have no right to personal feelings or desires, because war is something quite real and our love and future together is somewhat intangible at the moment especially. I know that it is selfish to even want a small part of you when you're needed for more important affairs—but Bruce, I honestly don't feel noble enough to give you up entirely to make the future safe for somebody else. That isn't a very patriotic attitude, is it? I'm selfish enough to want any little part of you—oh, it is so hard to try to explain anything in a letter—you can grasp the meaning of what I'm trying to say. Perhaps I don't quite understand what you mean about waiting.

Since I've been worrying and making my own resources I've learned quite a bit about what it takes to live on—also a lot about people and what makes them click—in short I suppose I've actually grown up and stopped seeing the world through rose colored spectacles—and sprees. It takes a lot of sacrifice to make complete happiness, of which you are fully aware—I hardly know how to say it—waiting takes a lot of patience and sacrifice I know and because of a little experience I haven't been very definite with you Bruce—experience in waiting I mean. Guess that involves a few "secrets" in my life that I do want to tell you but can't seem to put down on paper. Waiting comes a lot easier when you're sure of what lies ahead and the person you're waiting with—this is getting so complicated! Wish I could stop here and ask you if you understood but I'm sure you don't. I hardly do myself.

Darling I guess I'd better take my fences as they come and maybe this letter will make a little sense. The main point is that you are the only person I've ever really wanted. I used to wish so hard that you might like me even a little and after so many years I gave up hope and it became just a wishful dream. That Wednesday night in Charlotte when you held my hand—even that little bit of attention made me happy. But I was so afraid that you didn't mean a thing by it—that perhaps you thought I was still the brat that was Skinny's sister, except a little more grown up. Then I discovered that you did care—well I never wanted to leave you for a moment but naturally all good things come to a standstill at least. Do you think that if I had waited all these years without so much as a single bit of encouragement, that I wouldn't wait a few more years, knowing that you loved me? War needn't change that—unless you are transferred to foreign service—and then what! Bruce to be perfectly frank and sincere—I'm like Harry—I think a little is better than none at all. I guess as far as being sensible you are right—it isn't the most practical thing to marry and then leave for an indefinite time. Maybe Harry and I are a couple of romantic kids but I think where your whole heart is concerned that it should be your guide and not your conscience. I suppose this war isn't going to give either of us a chance—we'll just have to wait and take whatever comes. Bruce I love you—so as long as you're going to be waiting with me I can forget selfishness and be sensible for a change. There doesn't seem to be much we can do now but wait.

(from letter #49)

Wednesday night (Dec. 10, 1941. Postmark unreadable)

Bruce dearest,

This is the world's weariest little girl—I've been Christmas shopping and there aren't words to explain my dislike for all those people that get in my way! I don't really dislike them but they are such a hindrance when you're in a hurry. After reading your letter for the fourth time I feel quite refreshed. Bruce it makes me so mad to think that I could have been receiving these splendid letters for so long and haven't just because we were both blind as bats! Why didn't you tell me you wrote such letters anyway? In fact-why didn't you tell me a lot of things and save a lot of wear and tear on my heart? Oh darling, why can't wishes ever come true? One did –maybe if I keep wishing long enough all of them will come true. You know, I am looking forward to Christmas but it is going to be so lonely without you. New Years is especially going to be dull—think I'll just go to bed so there won't be occasion for wishful thinking.

(from letter #50)

Oakland Airport, Oakland, Calif. (Dec. 12, 1941)

Lu, you mentioned again that you were afraid that something would happen to ruin our happiness. Darling, it will never be anything that I am responsible for. Why do you feel like that? It makes me afraid, too.

I can't know how you are going to take this new situation until you tell me, and you must tell me you know. I'm not telling you this because I'm so terribly lonesome for you; because I miss you more now than I thought possible. Lu, I just can't conceal my feelings from you, nor do I want to. I wish that we could be married. Darling I want that more than anything. I have so many regrets about our past. Why did I have to wait all these years to discover that I felt this way? Now my problem is to convince you that we can hope for a future. You are still looking forward to next summer, and I hope that you still are. I realize what the war may mean, but it mustn't change things for us. I won't rest until I know how you feel about it.

It seems a long time to me, too, since we were together—sitting before the fire. Darling, I was never happier before in my whole life than when we were together, and I knew that I loved you, and that you cared for me. That memory I shall always cherish. If it only could have lasted longer. But neither do I want to make you blue. In spite of what has happened these past few days, I'm still not really unhappy. Just having your love makes all the difference, regardless of time or distance

Let me tell you something about this place. Actually, I can't say anything about our operations here, but there isn't much to say anyway. Lu, this will surprise you, and I hate to admit it, but our present set up is something you read about in books. I'm living in a hotel right beside the flying field. We have steam-heated rooms and a private bath. Harry and I are living together, as usual. Things have been much easier for us since Sunday than before, because of the way we are set up here to operate. We have an excellent mess, and there is absolutely nothing lacking. Well, I'm wrong again for that will never be true for me until I can have you with me.

There have been one or two bad moments—like for instance the first night or two when we had several air raid alarms and black outs. Perhaps you read about that in the paper. I was afraid that you would be frightened by some of the things you read, but don't be. Although there were supposed to have been a large group of enemy planes over San Francisco the other night, it is rather strange that if they were, they left again without doing a thing. I'll never believe there were any. But it had the West Coast all excited. There is a lot of war hysteria at a time like this, especially in the beginning. It was such a surprise in the first place. But our Navy and our Army over there seem to be getting control of the situation now. So don't you worry, darling. This just is an unpleasant experience we're going thru and there is an end to it ahead.

(from letter #52)

Sunday night (postmark Monday, Dec. 15, 1941)

Hello again,

You should be thankful to be in sunny California now. I sit wrapped up like an Eskimo at home and at school I hug the radiator—and still freeze. Guess I need my love to keep me warm!

You know, I've relived those few days we were together a hundred times—and it's still amazing. I've often wondered what might have happened that Wednesday night if I had gone on home without calling you. I really thought about it because I just knew you were being nice to "Skinny's sister"—and that would certainly put a damper on my holiday spirits. We didn't have much time together when it's all added up (even the wee hours included) but it was something, and I've existed on those few memories and your letters since you left.

(from letter #54)

Tuesday night (Dec. 16; postmark Dec. 17, 1941)

My dearest Lu,

Darling, I keep reading your letters, and find things that I forgot to answer, or mention. For instance you said that you were afraid of what was going to happen to us now that the war had started. Lu, I hope that by now I've talked you out of being worried about that. And darling don't say that you might find out you are dreaming about us. This is the most real thing that has ever happened to me. I think that it seems unbelievable because of the way it happened. Lu, it could have happened the first time I saw you again, and I'm so glad that it was possible then. I've told you this already but I want to tell you again— that I wanted very much to see you and yet I was afraid that it would be the same way as it was before. Remember when I first saw you in the bus station? I wanted to kiss you then, but perhaps you wouldn't have survived the shock. I think I would have been afraid to anyway. It took being away so long to make me realize that I loved you. To know that you cared for me, was such a surprise that I could hardly believe it, either. Can't we make up for that? I wish I could know what lies ahead, even just a little way, for, Lu, I know now what you want. I do, too, darling, and I am glad you told me how you felt. Except that I feel I'm not being fair with you if you really want us to be married soon. I'm trying so hard to be practical for both of us, for I know deep down in my heart it is best. Now I must convince you of that, too. Whatever happens to us, I don't want you to be unhappy ever. Here I always end up trying to make you understand how I feel. Darling, to have you say you will wait for me, makes me happy. If you love me that much, I don't deserve it but I'm selfish too, and I want your love.

Lu, my asking you to wait, isn't so much, or rather isn't at all because I feel we haven't a right to our personal desires now. You see I'm disagreeing with what you thought I meant. I'm still only thinking of the future for us—for you particularly. It's not a matter of our wanting our happiness as opposed to my having a war to fight. I'm thinking of your future, darling, and I can't make up my mind that you are right and I am wrong. What happiness we could have for a short time—full of uncertainty—wouldn't last a life time. I wonder if we will ever be able to see ahead to a time when there is something certain. Darling it's bad enough to have an aviator for a husband but it's even worse to have him in a war.

If I didn't think that this war would be short, I believe that I could forget my feelings about you and my one wish not to ever make you unhappy because of me. You see, I'm trying to tell you that I believe it selfish of me to want you now Lu, to realize a little happiness. After your letter, I don't know what to think, exactly. You don't agree with me do you? My writing isn't making good sense either, and maybe I'll have to translate for you.

Still, Lu, you are seeing my side of it, and are willing to wait. I don't deserve anyone to love me so much, if I can't meet them half way. I love you with all my heart, darling, and I always will. Don't ever doubt that, promise me. And I can't express what it means to me to have you love me, and to know that you will wait for me. I have something to live for, and hope for, and that will mean more than you can realize. Lu, we're going to be optimistic—see?

(from letter #58)

The letter that came next was tucked into the envelope of a letter from Bruce mailed on December 17, 1941. Frances never finished it and obviously never mailed it. She wanted to tell him more about her relationship with Charlie, but just could not bring herself to do it. She had probably not told Charlie about Bruce yet either. And incidentally, she never told me or my siblings about Charlie until decades had passed.

Bruce dearest,

First I want you to know that I love you (as if I hadn't told you)—no matter what happens, there will always be my love for you. All my life it seems I've been with people so much older than me—and perhaps I've felt that there was a certain stage I'd skipped, meaning dances, house parties etc. Guess I was childish enough to want these things when they add up to so little importance. At any rate when I went to summer school, I had that fun and it lasted almost two years—that's when teaching took up my spare time and there wasn't time for all those frolics. After I graduated there wasn't much interest left for the people my own age because most of them were still in school. Naturally our mutual interests lagged and with the aid of distance and time, there just wasn't any romance to it anymore. (All this is really leading up to something if you'll just follow me.)

Remember when we had a few true confessions and I told you I was afraid to tell you about a certain rumor you'd heard? I was and still am—afraid that you'll misunderstand and think as Mother does that I'm still a rather scatterbrained child who hasn't yet grown up. (Mothers never let their children grow up). All this goes back to the med student. You see, it was taken for granted by both of us, that when he finished his third year of med school that we would be married (remember the letter I wrote you about not teaching more than two years?) I've known for a long time I didn't love him and that his medical career was more important than I'd ever be—which I suppose was right—but I'm just not built that way. I want all or nothing—that is, with consideration for conventional things. Bruce I've loved you for so long—so long in fact that it became a kind of fairy tale that I knew could never come true and it took the unexpectedness of the way it happened to make me realize it actually had come true and there was no longer a need for me to pretend to myself that I could ever be completely happy with anyone else. Can you understand how I feel Bruce? I know you don't…

(The letter abruptly ends here. From letter #59, never sent to Bruce)

Home Friday night (Dec. 19; postmark Dec. 20, 1941)

My dearest Bruce,

Mom wanted to visit the antique shops *(in Charlotte, where they shopped frequently)* so we diddled away two good hours there—by that time Dad was so hungry he couldn't wait to drive home, so we had dinner at the S&W and took our time coming home. Since then Mom and I have caught up on gossip at both ends—and she is most curious about a certain fellow in the Air Corps. I'm really having a time keeping a secret. It isn't that I don't want Mother to know, it's just that I don't know how to tell her. You can't just say—I'm in love with Bruce—although I guess she should know by now since I haven't talked about anyone else since we left McBee this afternoon. She surely did appreciate your letter. Poor Mom—she has a time keeping up with her sons.

Do you know that if you had kissed me that day in the bus station—well, I really think I would have fainted. You're a fine one for shocking people anyway. Why, when you shook my hand I was so upset I could hardly make decent introductions. To say nothing of that Wednesday night at the airport—I was talking a blue streak and you took my hand. I didn't even know what I said after that. Good night, Bruce.

Love forever,

Lu

(from letter #62)

The question about whether to marry or not to marry went on apace. It was all about unfairness and uncertainty and practicality.

Monday night (Dec. 29, postmark Jan. 2, 1942)

My dearest Lu,

Lu, even after I told you that I loved you, I didn't dare think that you could love me enough to give up your life for mine. I don't think that I could give you what you were accustomed to, and what you deserved, and so didn't feel that I could make you happy. To ask you to share my life and my problems, or even to wait until I felt that I could provide for you, was more than I could ask of you. After all, what happened to us was rather sudden, and I didn't know if it were real or not. I know you didn't either, Lu.

Darling, you don't know what it would mean—being married to me. I haven't tried to tell you all this before, because I haven't told you even that I would ask you to marry me. Now that we both know something of how each other feels, I want to tell you. It's only right that I should. I'm being very frank and facing the facts, as you say you have been learning to do. Lu, coming out here to be with me would mean giving up your entire past life, family, and friends—all you've ever had and been used to. And it would be for good. It's happened to me, and although I don't think the Army has changed me much, it has definitely taken me away from all I ever knew before. It hasn't been hard for me and I've not regretted it, but it would be a tremendous readjustment for you. As I say, this is even more true with us at war. The way things are now, we couldn't even be together for long periods. Even now my duties require my presence from 8 to 12 hours every day and every 3rd night I'm on duty and can't leave the field.

There is always the possibility of me being sent out of the United States. Darling, I've been optimistic about this, and I still am, but the possibility remains, and it is a strong one. I could stand being away from you, but it would be so unfair to go away and leave you. Lu there isn't any reason why we shouldn't have all this out now. If I should leave the chances aren't 100% that I would ever come back. Have you thought about these things? I couldn't bear the thought of leaving you with that facing us, but it might come, and if so, it would be so much easier for you if we weren't married. Darling, I believe that to be true, and I think it is so, even if you might not agree with me. When I say I could stand being away from you, I mean I could take it a lot better knowing that you would be here when I came back, and knowing that I wasn't leaving you with the possibility of what might happen if I didn't come back at all, and we were married. That doesn't express my idea like I wanted it to. What I'm trying to say is, "Would it be worth it, having each other for perhaps only a very short while when we've counted on a lifetime?"

My darling, are you wondering what has come over me, writing like this? I'm just trying to show you what we're up against. You have said that you had no right to consider your personal happiness. But you are wrong. You have every right to that, and I'm trying to make you consider it—not for the present, and the way you may feel now, but for the very, very, long future ahead.

I can be happy knowing that you love me and that perhaps someday we will have a future. At least I think I can be but sometimes it isn't that way. When you tell me that you don't want to wait for us to be married, and that a little happiness is better than none, then I begin to feel the same way. Your feelings are mine too, and your desires are my concern. I love you,

Lu

(from letter #71)

In a rare display of frankness, Bruce was honest about the dangers he faced as a pilot.

Saturday night (Jan. 3, 1942, postmark unreadable)

My dearest,

We had a black-out tonight for about an hour—sent planes up, too, but they found nothing. It's the first we've had in some time and probably resulted from unidentified airplanes in the vicinity—friendly most likely. Since we are all fixed up for it, we just let the blinds down and go right on with the poker game or what not. Otherwise, there hasn't been much excitement. We had another fatal crash yesterday, though I had thought that I wouldn't mention it, but then you will have to get used to such things and there is no reason why I should try to keep you unexposed to the realities of my existence. This was a new inexperienced pilot, and we think he lost control of the plane while doing acrobatics and dived into the ground. I can't see anything but pilot error but of course we will never know exactly what happened. It is unpleasant, Lu, and we forget all about it immediately so it's forgotten.

Lu, I can see you just as though you were here. No, I haven't been drinking—but I have such a clear memory of how you looked that Sunday nite—the last one we had together. You were probably too tolerant with me that day and I keep remembering how I took you back so late.

Goodnight darling. I dreamed I went home the other night, and how surprised you were when you saw me! I kissed you and before either of us could speak I woke up. I wonder what you were about to say. Can you tell me?

I love you,

Bruce

(from letter #74)

Saturday (Jan. 10 1942, postmark Jan. 12)

Bruce, I've been trying to answer your long letter and my efforts have been in vain because I was sure you would misunderstand me. You are right about most things you spoke of—I've just been afraid to even believe I've thought there was ever a possibility of your having to leave and perhaps never return—it hurts to think these things without putting them down in black and white.

It seems you and I are both pretty obstinate in our views on our futures. You've asked "would it be worth it loving each other for perhaps a very short while, when we've counted on a lifetime?" You already know my answer to that. Perhaps I can explain what I mean like this. When I think of all the years we have known each other and yet have not known what the other really felt—well, I believe that if I suddenly realized that I'd never see you again or that perhaps you discovered it wasn't as real as you thought, then I could be better satisfied and even a little happy with the thought that I had had a few days of complete happiness with you. In my own crude way this seems to be the same as being married to you for always with the uncertainty of what might and could happen. Guess I'm still the romantic kid and not very practical but still I can't see all of your views.

Perhaps I should stick to my slap-happy theories and when I get too senseless just let you pull me out of the clouds with a little practical advice. Although my arguments would have been so much better before this war I'm afraid I can't compete with your sensible nature and uncertainty.

I can set my foot down very firmly on some of the things you said though. Just what kind of a person do you think I'd be if I didn't love you enough to share all of your joys and sorrows, troubles and responsibilities anywhere on this earth you might be! That dark picture you painted about leaving all my friends, family etc. for an entirely new life just doesn't discourage me one bit, Lieut. Parcell, because you see, I happen to be more than just fond of you which makes it necessary for my happiness for me to be with you.

(from letter #81)

Wednesday night (Jan 21, 1942 postmark Jan. 23)

My dearest Lulu,

You asked about my pet hates, etc. Lu, as far as you are concerned I haven't any, except that I want you to be more outspoken about what you feel and think. Like your telling me that you didn't know whether to call me or not that evening in Charlotte. I don't want to ever feel you won't tell me exactly what you want to. Nothing you could say would change the way I feel about you, for that feeling isn't based on our few days together, but all our lives, and what you are and have always been. Lu, you're the only girl I've ever known that I thought was too good for me. I know you don't approve of an idea like that, but it's true. That is another reason I don't want to hurt you. Darling, I never thought that you could ever love me. I don't know why. Then to discover otherwise kind of frightened me because I felt we might not ever have each other and be happy together. I can't explain that either.

Until the past year I've never even been able to think of marriage, and even then I didn't think of it because there was no one in my life that I'd ever gone with who I would have asked to marry me. Darling I did tell Harry about you, and that you were my ideal. I never realized that someday you would love me. My dearest, you are my ideal. I'll always think of you that way. Lu, you always seemed so far away before—so distant. I know—perhaps that was my fault. It was my loss, too, for now I have to make love to you by long distance mail. That's bad when I want you so very much. Sometimes I think it's wrong to want you so. Darling, do you know I actually felt I'd done something wrong when I first kissed you. Because I thought you didn't want me to. I actually thought you just tolerated it because it was me and we had known each other for so long.

Say, this is getting to be quite a true confession or something, isn't it?

Well, I still haven't told you tonight that you are the sweetest person in the world, and that I love you more than I've told you. And that someday you're going to be my wife, if you'll have me then.

For always and always,

Bruce

(from letter #92)

Frances wrote this letter to follow up on a rare telephone conversation. She tried very hard to be outspoken and to counter Bruce's arguments about waiting to get married.

Sunday night (Jan. 25, 1942 postmark Jan. 27)

My sweetheart,

All day Saturday I kept thinking of things I wanted to say when you called and then when I heard your voice, everything escaped my thoughts except that you were actually talking to me and Bruce, it just meant more to me than I can say. Please forgive me for being so unsuccessful in my attempts to say what I wanted to say.

Your call was the way of letting Mom in on our secret. Bruce I'm afraid my emotions betrayed me but I'm glad because now Mother knows how I feel about you and she is truly glad—it seems there are a lot of inner thoughts being brought to light—she'd been hoping for this thing to happen, I firmly believe. She told me a lot of nice things to tell you, but I think I'll just be mean and not even mention them--now a dose of your own medicine! I wanted to pay a visit to your mother while I was home but I guess I'm a little shy without you. I saw Sarah today and I told her I'd talked to you—she wanted to know if you called all the way from California. She's sweet Bruce—her facial expressions and certain mannerisms remind me of you.

You know, I'd hate to start an argument now when time is so short, but when you say things like, "it would be best for me not to make a sacrifice by marrying you now and then perhaps never being able to enjoy a lifetime of happiness with you"—well Bruce—don't you see that there'll never be another you? Don't you see that there could never

ever be anyone to fill your place in my heart? My love for you isn't just a make believe dream—it's real and very strong and neither time nor person could make me feel any differently. Dearest, you aren't just the person I've dreamed of as my Prince Charming (every girl actually has one)—you're the person I've hoped for as a companion for any happiness or sorrow that might come. There are probably a lot of people I could say would make anybody a wonderful lover, but I think there's more to being in love than just talking about it. Bruce, you're the only person in this world I could ever want for a lifetime companion. Does that explain in any way why I feel so determined about having a small share in your life even in this time of uncertainty? You want me to be more outspoken, so I shall—I suppose this is the main reason I'm so obstinate about our future—you see, I would be very patient and wait for the "someday" if I could assure myself there would be a "someday," but somehow it's hard to take such a long chance and that's why I'm so insistent about a little being better than nothing. Do you understand?

Forever yours,

Lu

(from letter #98)

Monday night (Jan.26, 1942 postmark Jan. 29, special delivery)

Darling, don't ever feel that you're not being fair to me. If I had never found that you loved me I would have dreamed my life away hoping still that maybe someday you would notice me. It is truly fantastic to realize you do love me and then you wonder about being fair to me. It makes me feel that I'm the one that should do the wondering, because it seems I'm making you unhappy writing you the things I do. It isn't a question of being fair Bruce—it wouldn't have been fair if you had loved me and never told me.

You know I have two very distinct pictures of you in my mind—this last snapshot reminds me very much of one---the Sunday night your brought me home. I don't believe I'll ever forget the way you looked when you kissed me goodbye. I knew somehow that we wouldn't see each other again before you returned to California. The snapshot, which I've looked at until I'm dizzy, has that certain very serious look. The other picture is the mischievous boy who makes me nearly burst with joy when he's in such a very slap-happy mood, as the earlier part of that Sunday night in Charlotte. To live that one day over would mean so much, but here now, I shouldn't start anything, because you might get angry with me and Bruce, I couldn't bear to have you think badly of me now. When you get really angry with me I want to be with you so that I won't have to wait through weeks of argument by mail to be forgiven.

Forever yours,

Lu

(from letter #99)

Sunday nite (February 1, 1942)

It's been a busy day for us. We are training the new pilots who joined the squadron not long ago, and it's some job. Some of them are pretty erratic and it is hard work flying with them .It's getting to be a joke now—the way we train new men and then have them transferred out again. We're almost a training squadron, whereas we were supposed to have been a first priority fighting unit. But I'm not complaining about it, for it keeps me here that much longer, and that means I still might get to see you.

This will surprise you. I have been recommended for promotion to a Captain. How about that? Of course, that's all there is to it and even if I get the promotion it would be temporary one—but just the same, I can't picture it, myself. If it goes thru I'll really have something to write home about.

Always,

Bruce

(from #104)

NORTH CAROLINA CALLING

With the news in this next letter, everything was about to change again. Bruce was being transferred from California to Wilmington, North Carolina, proving that sometimes dreams do come true. He would be coming home, at least for a while.

Friday Night (Feb. 6, 1942 postmark Feb. 7)

Hi, little tough girl!

This is going to be short—but you won't believe it, I'll bet. For a year and a half now I have wondered if I would ever get any nearer home. Now it's coming to be a fact instead of a hope. Lu, I'll be in Wilmington, N.C., a permanent change of station, within about two weeks. How about that? It's unbelievable almost. I don't know whether I should tell you or not until later, but after all you aren't a Fifth Columnist or a Nazi spy. Wilmington isn't the best spot in N.C.—but it is North Carolina, and I'm not complaining in the least. And this isn't something that might fall through because it is definite now. The only thing that might upset it is the fact that my name did get on a list for something else. That has been a few weeks ago though, and nothing has been said about it to me as yet by anyone. So I'm hoping that is all off. You can hope for me. So, Lu, I will be seeing you—soon—I'm sure.

Be sweet, darling, and remember that I'm looking forward to seeing you, because I love you and have missed you more than is good for me. It won't be long until I can say I'll see you tomorrow.

Always,

Bruce

(from letter #109)

Sunday night (Feb. 8, 1942 postmark Feb. 9)

Hello Santa Claus!

You can never know how that bit of good news has set me off—I feel a spree coming on. Hope something doesn't bring me down to earth again because it's such fun anticipating a possible chance of seeing you again and soon. I've already learned to expect the worst from the Army though. One never knows!

Now see here Lieut. Parcell—you're just getting too high in the world for me to reach you. Captain indeed! Why I won't be able to speak to you without feeling like one of the lowly worms. (I hope you get the promotion though). I guess I'd love you even if you were a Captain. As you say I guess it's a nice thought anyway.

I'm holding my breath until I hear from you again—

For always—

Lu

(from letter #112)

Finally, in the waning days of February of 1942, Frances and Bruce had their long awaited reunion. Both wrote letters immediately after their time together. It must not have gone as anticipated because both expressed unhappiness with the weekend. They had poured out their innermost feelings on paper for months, and expectations for this meeting were high. Neither of them felt that they had been able to say the things they really felt once they were face to face again. Letters that followed Bruce's move to Wilmington indicate that when they were together, they argued quite a bit. It doesn't take much reading between the lines to understand why. Frances wanted to get married; Bruce wanted to wait. She clearly felt that if he loved her as much as he said he did, marriage would be the obvious next step. Neither of them sounded happy with the status quo. Here are the first letters they exchanged after their weekend together:

Sunday night (March 1, 1942 postmark March 2)

My dearest Bruce,

Call it guilty conscience or maybe lonesomeness but I have a very uneasy feeling. Bruce I love you and I want to help make you happy, but I feel that these past two days have been complete failures in that respect. I've actually been scolding myself all day because I was so dull this weekend and I had wanted your homecoming to be the best.

Here I've been wishing I could see you so I could talk to you only to have my wish come true and then not be able to say the things I wanted to say. Isn't that dumb!

I'm not going to be worth one thing at school this week. My mind isn't in California either! I'll never stop wishing I could see you. I can hardly wait until you write and tell me if I might come this weekend. Regardless of whether they fire me for going off so much, I'm coming to see you if I can persuade you to let me. I promise not to be serious a single time and I'll even do exactly what you say (maybe). Anything to make up for being such a prude this weekend.

I love you Bruce—and I surely do miss you—already.

Yours always

Lu

(from letter #117)

Wilmington, N.C., March 2, 1942

Dearest Lu,

Lu, it was so good to see you again. But like you said, there wasn't much to say, and somehow I couldn't talk to you either. I know it's all my fault, too. Perhaps it would have been better if I had gone *(overseas)* from the coast, since things are like they are. I don't know, Lu, I'm all confused and mixed up, too. But still I think I'm right and I can't help feeling that way. Somehow I don't even want to talk about it. But maybe I'll be able to when I see you again. We aren't going to be too busy for a while and as it is now we have every other night free. I have off on odd nights and can be out until 12:00 midnight on even days if I get someone to take my place. So I will be able to see you more than 10 minutes. And you now have a formal invitation to come to Wilmington—from Harry and Toni. They have a house near the field. So I'll be looking for you when you decide to come. Wire me at the airport and I'll meet you in town.

Lu, I do want you to come down but I'll leave it up to you whether this weekend or next. Whatever suits you best. Be sweet, and I'll be seeing you.

Love,

Bruce

(from letter #118)

Wilmington, N.C., Wednesday Evening (March 4, 1942 postmark March 5)

Dearest Lu,

What can I say except that I'm as sorry as can be that you felt so badly about our weekend. Your letter came this morning and it was good to find something to break the monotony of camp life, Boy Scout style. Yes, I suppose our reunion was more or less a bust, but don't blame yourself, Lu, for it wasn't your fault at all. You were very sweet considering what you had to put up with. Truly, this war has gotten me "off the beam" and I'm lapsing into some of those moods I warned you about. You are right. Thinking too much isn't a good thing. And what I need is to get back to some hard work so I won't have the opportunity. However, I feel that when you come down to see me, we can at least talk sensibly. I promise to do better. But, if I'm still in the dog house—I don't know. Of course, I know you have a right to that, but it makes me awfully unhappy. Lu, I have a feeling that I've not added any to your happiness, and the one thing that I never want to do is to hurt you. You deserve something better than that. I've tried to tell you that before, you know. But I'll tell you all about it again, when I see you. I hope you will come this weekend, Lu, and even if we can't be together except Sat. night, I know we can do better than before. Lu, I miss you too, already.

I flew a P-39 this morning for the first time. It is going to be O.K. and I know we will like it later on. This noon we had a squadron party—barbecued ribs and beer—can you imagine? Anyway, we make the best of life.

Our camp is close to the field here, and we have floors in the tents—and stoves. It's very comfortable and anyway it isn't long till summer time. I'm not making any plans—it's going to be nice on the beach I'm sure.

Please don't be worried, Lu. I love you—in spite of whatever I do or say. Write to me, will you? See you Saturday.

As ever,

Bruce

(letter #119)

Bruce tried to call but the terrible telephone situation in McBee prevented communication. The Mr. Sexton of whom she speaks was the owner of the gas station where McBee's lone telephone resided.

Sat. night (March 7, 1942 postmark March 9)

My dearest Bruce,

I don't think I've ever been so angry in all my life! I've counted up to fifty to keep from saying what I said anyway. This ___ ___ town and its modern conveniences!! It seems you called me tonight at seven o'clock and I didn't get the message simply because I

Mr. Sexton's McBee Motor Company, also a gas station and the location of the only telephone in town.

didn't happen to be in sight when the call came through. As soon as I got your second message at ten o'clock (fifteen minutes after your call came through) I tried for an hour and a half to get you back but with no success. Bruce I'm so very disappointed—it would have been such a grand surprise to talk to you. I tried to call the airport and they said all telephones had been disconnected so of course 'ole imagination started playing tricks again but maybe I'll hear from you tomorrow and everything will be okay. Bruce, I'm so upset I can't think of another thing but how provoked I am with Mr. Sexton. It just took all my will power to keep from telling him to go jump in a lake! This town is so lazy you couldn't excite them with an air raid.

I've been terrible about writing this week but there's been a rush from morn till night. My banquet was—well, I guess you'd say a success, but at any rate we had a good time. Even if we did have to work all day and half the night. After the banquet we stayed at the school house getting things back to order (you surely can make a terrific mess in a very short time) then at twelve o'clock I started my taxi service. One child told me she lived "just a little ways from here"—well, I drove twenty miles on the highway, five on a dirt road and heaven only knows how many on the most "back woodsy" path I've ever traveled—and in the middle of the night with only three "brave" girls for protection. Had I known what I know now that child would have spent the night in my bed and I would gladly have rocked myself to sleep in the rocker. I was so busy keeping in the road etc. that I didn't have time to realize what an awkward situation I would have been in if a tire had blown out while we were there in the middle of nowhere. I've had ample thinking time today though—never again! She said the place where she lived was called the "Head of the Nog—Eleven devils and nary a god." I truly believe her.

I love you Bruce—and because I do, I'll be very sensible and agreeable next time we meet.

For always

Lu

(from letter #121)

There were some lighter notes mixed in with all the agonizing over who was to blame for making them both unhappy when they met in Wilmington. While she was there one weekend, Frances had found some silly telegraph forms at the Western Union office with funny comments and check-boxes on them, and she had written some extra comments. She left them anonymously in Bruce's car. "Here is a big X and a big round O, a kiss and a hug for one I love so," and "I will kiss you if I can because you have been so very good, and I love you" were messages on one of them. The other one sported an X mark by the comment, "Here's for that smashing finish when you turn on the heat." Indeed! He scolded her teasingly about this, calling her a rascal and threatening to spank her.

After about a month of Bruce's trying to convince Frances that marriage was out of the question, she wrote this.

Friday afternoon At School (March 27, 1942 postmark March 27)

My dearest,

Can you picture an empty classroom with very lonely teacher doing a "heap of remembering?" That's me exactly. The children have all gone and I've no one to keep me company except the mice in the kitchen. I've just read your letter and although it was a tremendous help, I'm still lonesome.

Another thing, Parcell—I would rather you wouldn't tell me how you feel about my being with you when it just gets us started on the same argument again. Perhaps you'll never see that, although I love you, I don't want to have you make promises and plans for a day that may and may not come. I love you and I wish I could tell the world but I haven't any right to tell anyone how I feel about you. As you say, there's nothing you can say when people inquire about the "fellow on the coast," a California car, "frequent letters from brother"—well I just change the subject and declare there's nothing to it. I certainly can't say I love him but he's going to war so that's that. Anyway it isn't that simple. I don't know—things are complicated for me too so perhaps we'd do well to forget the whole thing and take life as it comes.

Forever yours,

Lu

(from letter #133)

His letter, written the next day, was interesting if you read between the lines even just a little bit. His resolve to postpone marriage seemed to be weakening.

Saturday Night (March 28, 1942 postmark March 28)

Lu, darling

Now see here, my sweet, even if you do want me to refrain from saying how I feel, I won't do it. And I won't attempt to forget anything either. Some things you can't forget. I love you, Lu, and I'll keep on telling you—and one of the first things you know, I'll surprise you—and tell you that I am not happy any longer when you are not with me. Lu, if I am not actually up flying, my work has gone to ___. My days aren't too bad, but after work, I get so lonesome. You spoiled me by being here two weekends and I was determined to see you. Still want to.

Lu, the more I think about it, the more I realize how much trouble I must have been. You really had a tough time of it while you were here, but then why do you suppose you did? Let's wait until I see you again, darling, for I have so much to tell you. I love you so, and I'm not going to let you forget it. I'm going to make up for all those unhappy moments you've spent on my account, because to feel that I've hurt you is like hurting myself. I meant that, Lu. There isn't going to be any argument, either, see, because I refuse to let it be.

Lu, did you feel terribly mad at me when you wrote Fri? Please don't, sweetheart, I can't stand it.

I love you with all my heart,

Bruce

Then, while it can only be inferred from what is in subsequent letters, Bruce must have given up on his arguments on the weekend of April 4-5, when he apparently decided marriage might not be such a bad idea after all. A marriage proposal was surely part of their time together. How that might have happened is lost to history. Here is Frances's first letter after that. She was investigating how to go about getting a marriage license.

Tuesday night (April 7, 1942 postmark unreadable)

My dearest,

To think this is only Tuesday—three whole long days until I can see you! Bruce I miss you so much—it would really be the sensible thing to wait until next weekend to go to Wilmington but I can't wait any longer—do you mind? Well, I don't care if you do—see!

Frank *(probably Frank Purdy, another Barium boy)* said he would go with me to get the license—it seems we don't have to sign it but we have to get it in the same county we're married in. We won't worry about the ushers just yet—that's your worry anyway! Mom keeps telling me not to worry about anything, which is useless. I'm not worrying. I just can't eat nor sleep. I just keep remembering how much I want to see you and how much I love you. Will Sat. ever come!

Yours always,

Lu

(from letter #138)

That very same day she wrote a second letter in which she was already making wedding plans. Such was the roller coaster nature of this remarkable romance. Five months before, she thought Bruce only had brotherly feelings towards her. Now marriage was in the offing, and soon.

In the midst of getting engaged, Bruce had to go to Orlando, Florida, to some sort of flight school. From there he wrote to both his mother and his future mother-in-law. He summed up in a few paragraphs what he and Frances had been writing about in dozens of lengthy letters.

Orlando, Florida, Tuesday night (no envelope; probably April 7, 1942)

Dear Mother,

It seems I never quite settle down in one place. When I got back, I had orders to come down here, and left Monday morning. I'm going to school, and will be here until around the 13th.

It is lovely here, with a fragrance of orange blossoms in the air. And not too hot yet. Sorry I didn't get to stay longer the other night. I went to church Sunday, and saw Sarah. It was the nicest Easter Sunday in a long long time.

Here I am talking very casually of other things, when I have something of special importance to tell you. As a matter of fact, you are probably going to be somewhat surprised, but I hope not too much so. Just remember that it isn't too unusual. Frances and I are going to be married. Perhaps you have had at least a faint suspicion of something, but I know hearing it now will surprise you. Mother, I've given it a lot of thought and that is what I want. For several reasons, I thought that I would wait awhile before making such a decision, but have finally reached the conclusion that it is useless to postpone it. And that's the way she wants it, too. Due to this trip, I will postpone my leave until the 25th and we will be married then at Barium. We haven't made plans yet, for it is a little uncertain about my leave.

I called Frances tonight, and she will be at home this weekend, and might go over to see you. I wish I could be at home now, but will have to wait. I want her to have everything just as she wishes it and I know that you will want it that way too.

I don't know what you're going to say, Mom, but now you know, anyway. I'd rather you not tell everyone now. Anyway, Frances said that her mother thought it best to have it announced, so it probably will be soon. As for me, I'm kind of in a spin at the moment, being down here.

Write me a special at the Army Air Base, Orlando, Fla, c/o Visiting Officers Quarters. It's late and I must close. Love to all, and I'll see you before so long.

Love,

Bruce

(letter #140)

Orlando, Florida, April 7, 1942 (postmark April 10, 1942)

Dear Mrs. Lowrance,

It is amazing what can happen when you least expect it. When I reached Wilmington I had orders waiting for me to go to Orlando to attend a school for a week. So, here I am, and it is really wonderful here.

I called Frances tonight and talked with her for a little while. And I promised I'd write to you, since I just couldn't quite get around to talking to you Sunday. Perhaps I was a little bit afraid to, but I did have good intentions. And now you already know. But I'll feel better if I tell you again myself. Even now I am at a loss as to what to say. For some time I've known that I wanted Frances to marry me, but only recently did I know that I didn't wish to postpone asking her. All along I have felt that it was unfair for me to even think of asking her to give up so much for what might be so little. We talked about that ever so much. I even wanted to talk to you about it before I asked her, but never did. I tried so long to reason with myself that I knew what was best for us, and that it would be better to wait. But I love her, and there is no reasoning that can change that. It is difficult for me to try to tell you how I feel, but I know that my life will never be quite complete without her. And I hope that we will have your blessing. If I can make her happy, I will not regret having married her in spite of the uncertainty of everything as it is since the war started.

I told Frances tonight that I could postpone my 10 day leave until the 25th of the month, and she thinks it better that way for it will give us more time. I should be back in Wilmington by the 13th or 14th. It is going to be rather difficult for her, for it seems she will have to do most of our planning. Things are so subject to change with me that I'm never definitely sure of any pre-arranged plans until the last minute. But I will call her from time to time between now and then. And I want her to have everything just as she wishes it.

My address here is Army Air Base, Orlando, Fla, c/o Visiting Officers Quarters. I can't tell you anything about my trip now, but will later. It's a military secret sure enough this time.

Love,

Bruce

(letter #141)

He also wrote to Frances:

Orlando, Florida, Tuesday Night (April 7, 1942 postmark April 8)

My darling,

It's terribly late and I have time only for a note, but I must write. It was so good to talk to you. It's the next best thing to having you here with me—and I've been wishing for that all day long. I love you so very very much, my dearest, and I'll be lonesome now until we are together again.

Have just written to your mother and mine too. So my mom will know. Lu, I couldn't have her read in the paper that we were to be married. That would be terrible, don't you think. But she will have my letter in a day or two.

Darling, I'm a fine person! Here you want our engagement announced, and you have no engagement ring. Things haven't turned out like I thought *(a small understatement)*. As a matter of fact, I don't know how such a situation could have been avoided as things have worked out. Listen, Lu, I will call you again Sat. nite at 7:30 at Barium. I'll make it a personal call so if you can't be there, leave word where to find you. Until then, I love you with all my heart.

For always,

Bruce

Frances's next letter was filled with exuberant and extravagant plans for the wedding. His reply bubbled over with happiness. Plus he announced that they would be living in Charlotte, at least for a little while.

Sunday night (April 12, 1942 postmark unreadable, maybe April 13)

My darling-

How long has it been since I've seen you! Bruce I'm so lonely without you even though I am so busy I don't know which end is up. You know I feel rather guilty in a way-doing all this planning without asking you—and underneath I know you don't want a big wedding and that's exactly what ours is going to be.

First thing—I shopped all day Sat. then went to Nina's *(Her brother Fred's girl friend)* Sat. night. The party was lovely and you've never seen such surprised people in all your life. Kat and Blanche were astonished but just as thrilled as I. I went up to see Kat and Frank *(Purdy)* today. Frank vowed and declared we were already married. I wish you were here to get in on the fun. It amuses me to see how surprised and shocked some people are. Mr. Cook *(the preacher at Little Joe's Church in Barium Springs)* just couldn't believe it. I told him we would talk to him later about the ceremony and such.

Next, you'd better prepare yourself. I'm having Anne as maid-of –honor; Ruth as matron-of-honor; Nancy and June; Leila and Winnie Pons and Winnie Shealy and Nina as bridesmaids—Sally as flower girl and "Butch" as ring bearer. Esther Love (one of my sorority sisters) is going to sing and Margaret Anne Costner, my cousin, is going to play. I've selected *The Rosary, Liebestraum,* and *Clair de Lune* to be played before the ceremony; *To a Wild Rose* during the ceremony. Esther Love is going to sing *Oh, Promise Me* and either *Because* or *I Love You Truly.* Have you any preferences? This is your wedding, too, although I haven't given you much say so.

Although it isn't necessary to have the same number of groomsmen as you do bridesmaids, we'll have to have enough to seat the people without having to rush. Did you ever decide who you wanted for best man? (that is a necessity.) I'd like Fred to be an usher—he is almost as excited as I am although he says he still thinks of me as being that high and not half old enough to get married. Tsk!

I do hope Skinny and Frankie can come up but I have my doubts. I would write Leonard but I don't know where he is. I went over to see your mother this morning. You really are in the dog house with me and Mrs. Parcell. Oh yes—did you write Blanche?—if you didn't your mother said it was your worry and she thought it should be done. So Parcell, you'd best get busy or Blanche will put you a little further back in the dog house.

Let me hear from you soon. I love you and Bruce, I miss you so very much. I hope it won't be long before I see you again.

Yours always,

Lu

(from letter #144)

Tuesday Night (April 14, 1942 postmark April 15)

My dearest sweetheart,

Talking to you tonight has made me happy—and lonesome. Lu, you mean so much to me now, and I miss you much too much if that is possible. Why aren't you here or I there right this minute? I don't know what I am going to do with myself until we are together again. When you come down Saturday, you're going to have a hard time getting away again. We've been apart for too long, you know.

Darling, I won't try to send you any names tonight. I just can't think straight. All I can think of is you, and how terribly much I want you with me.

O yes, the good news! Well I think we are going to move to the Air Base at Charlotte soon. That's the dope now and if it isn't changed, we should be there within the next ten days or two weeks. Perhaps before my leave starts, anyway. I'll let you know as soon as I find out anything. If we do go, the chances are good that we will be there all summer.

You know, Lu, It's still hard to believe that we are planning things together. It's like a dream, and I hope I never wake up. We do have a lot of plans, and we must see each other to work them out.

I don't know who to have for best man, Lu. It's really a problem for me. I doubt if Harry can be there, so I don't know what I'll do. But we'll talk about all this Sat., I hope. Right now I'm content to say I adore you, that you're a little _ _, that I am so happy and that I love you more than I thought was possible.

So don't worry, my darling, and don't work too hard. We'll have our wedding and it will be wonderful. I kind of think I'll like it, too, see? At any rate, I have an idea I'll be around to see what happens. Would you like that?

Do you think I'm crazy? I am but I can't help it. It seems a certain young lady I know has an awful lot to do with it. Oh, Lu, I love you so, and that is the most wonderful thing that ever happened to me.

Always,

Bruce

You're kind of cute too. Do you mind if I sort of remind you just once more that I love you with all my heart?

(from letter #145)

A letter to Blanche, straightforward as always, carried an alarming note about the unpredictability of Army life.

Friday night (postmark Sat. April 18, 1942)

Dearest Blanche,

Well, we leave Wilmington next week and are moving to Charlotte, which will make it nice for me. My leave starts on the 30th, and Frances will also take some leave. We are to be married at Barium on May 2nd. Other than that I can't tell you much, because I've been away so much I haven't been able to keep in touch with what is going on. Frances is coming down tomorrow afternoon, so I'll soon know what is cooking. She wants a church wedding and it will probably be a rather elaborate affair.

Yes, it's hard for me to believe yet. For I somehow can't picture myself married. This isn't the best time either, for such a step, but we've both considered all this, and so, you have the answer. To even try to predict what will happen to me in the future is foolish. I've postponed the idea several times already because of the uncertainty of the future and now we're just taking a chance. Just yesterday, a bunch of us were told to pack our bags for a secret move, a permanent change of station, and at the last minute only three went. It was too close for comfort, now that our plans have gone so far. So I won't rest easy until my leave starts, and the 2nd arrives.

Love,

Bruce

(from letter #146)

On April 19, Frances wrote about her new engagement ring. Bruce must have given it to her on the weekend of April 17-18 when she visited Wilmington. In later years she liked to tell the story of going back to McBee on the bus wearing it for the first time. She kept admiring it and knew that everyone on the bus noticed it because it was the most beautiful ring she had ever seen. In that story, though, she never mentioned how talk of marriage had been going on for months, nor that the wedding was already mostly planned.

> Bruce I've looked at the ring so long and so hard that I'm dizzy. It is just exactly right and I know there isn't a prettier one anywhere. Think I'll start drinking milk and gain weight so it will fit. Guess it will be okay when the weather gets a little warmer. Bruce I love you—so much that I can never tell you enough.
>
> Yours forever,
>
> Lu

(from letter #147)

Then came this from Leila, mother-in-law to be:

April 20. 1942

> Dearest Bruce,
>
> I did appreciate you writing to me. I might have helped along a little if I had known you wanted to talk to me. But it is just as well for I would rather you and Frances would decide for yourselves. I know you are going to be happy and you do have our blessing. Frances is our baby but I would rather give her to you than to anyone I know. If you are as good to her as her father has been to me I will never regret saying that.
>
> Let us know if there is anything you want done before you come.

Lots of love,

Leila Mc Lowrance

(from letter #149)

One last letter went to Wilmington from McBee before the wedding. D.B. was another recalcitrant student who seems to have had a romantic interest in his teacher.

Monday night (April 20, 1942 postmark April 21?)

My dearest,

What a time I've had today. Every child at school that hadn't seen the announcement in the paper found out about it two minutes before I arrived and I've spent my day explaining when, why, what, and where-fore! Every time I'd turn my back someone would drop a note on my desk wishing us luck and happiness—they even pinned notes on the other classroom desks and hid them in my coat pocket. I don't know the reason for all the secrecy unless they just hate to admit writing such. Poor D.B.—he's trying so hard to dishearten me. He's done noth-

Mr. and Mrs. Jay Hepburn Lowrance
request the honour of your presence
at the marriage of their daughter
Leila Frances
to
Bruce Farley Parcell
Lieutenant, United States Army Air Corps
on Saturday evening, the second of May
at eight-thirty o'clock
Little Joe's Presbyterian Church
Barium Springs, North Carolina

ing today but say "please don't get married, Miss Lowrance"—in fact he informed me that school teaching was much more fun than getting married. The kids are blaming all of this on you—they think you've led me astray. Tsk, tsk—"Mr. Parnell certainly has caused a lot of trouble!" I kinda like this kind of trouble—isn't that strange?

(from letter #150)

With the wedding date set, a whirlwind of activity ensued. There may have been a war going on but it did not dampen anyone's spirits. On Monday night before the wedding, a group of Barium ladies hosted a bridal shower at Rumple Hall, the huge dining hall on the orphanage campus. There were thirty-three guests, who played games and had dessert before a "youthful aviator" arrived with airplane luggage filled with gifts.

On Tuesday, Mrs. Frank Purdy, one of the Barium matrons *(Frank Purdy's mother)*, gave a bridge party at her home. Then on Wednesday Frances's friends June Burks and Anne Branan entertained for her in Charlotte, where about twenty college friends gathered. This was also a shower, with household linens as the theme.

Not to be outdone, Frances's mother and her sister Ruth gave a tea at the Lowrance home in Barium Springs. The last "prenuptial honor" was a cake cutting on Friday night following the wedding rehearsal. This party, given by Frances's Uncle Gus and his wife Teresa, included about forty guests. Frances wore a red and white chiffon dress with a full skirt, fitted bodice, and sweetheart neckline. The decorations were quite fancy and elaborate.

Some Of War Planes Over Statesville Were Serenading Lovers

Some of the war planes seen frequently over Statesville and vicinity in recent days were on a mission of love rather than war, it is reported here.

They were comrades serenading Lieutenant Bruce Parcell at his home in Cleveland and his bride, Miss Frances Lowrance, at her home in Barium Springs.

In other words they were love birds dipping their wings in felicitation to the bridal couple rather than eagles preening themselves for a fight.

This little article appeared in the Statesville Daily Record, *probably the week before the wedding.*

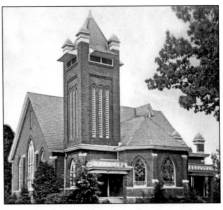

Little Joe's Presbyterian Church.

The wedding took place at Little Joe's Church in Barium Springs at 8:30 in the evening. As noted in one of the letters, Anne Branan, Frances's best friend,

Mama Kate Parcell, Bruce and Frances, and Leila Lowrance in front of famous rock fireplace in the Lowrance home during the wedding reception

Anne Branan, Bruce and Frances, and Harry Gillett during the wedding reception

was the maid of honor, her sister Ruth matron of honor. There were six other bridesmaids, a ring bearer, and a flower girl, Bruce's little niece Sally Graham. Sally was his older sister Katherine's daughter.

Frances's mother designed the wedding gown, which was made of satin, white net, and Chantilly lace. The many bridesmaids' dresses were alike in design but different in color: yellow, blue, pale pink, dark pink, and rose pink. It was, as Bruce had anticipated in his letter to Blanche, "quite an elaborate affair."

The reception was held at the Lowrance home in Barium. Frances and Bruce were able to go on a short honeymoon before both of them had to go back to work. They went to Greensboro where they stayed in the O. Henry Hotel downtown and took a picture of the First Presbyterian Church. Bruce returned to Charlotte, not Wilmington, for during the third week of April he was relocated to Morris Field. Frances returned to McBee to give tests and grade papers.

MARRIED LIFE

Once they were married and settled down, Bruce and Frances had few occasions to write to each other. Their story is harder to trace. But when they were apart, they wrote to each other. What follows are the letters between May 2, 1942, their wedding day, and February 14, 1944, when Bruce was sent first to New York and then overseas.

Frances left a letter somewhere for Bruce to find just a week after the wedding. It was her first letter as his wife. They had been corresponding for so long that it must have seemed natural for her to write in this way, even though they were now together. Written on the outside of the envelope was "Married One Week."

May 9, 1942

Dear Lieut. Parcell,

I just want to thank you for the very delightful husband you gave me for a wedding gift. He is really the nicest person I've ever known—considering everybody!

How can I tell you in so many words that I love him more than anything and although he's probably a very essential object at the air base (and naturally I wouldn't have him neglect his work) I do miss having him around to tease and talk to. He's a perfect companion—or did you know that before you gave him up?

I used to think he was kinda queer but now he's just outstanding—in fact I'm so proud to be his wife that I'm floating on air.

I also want to thank you, Lieut. Parcell, for giving me such a quaint name-- don't you like "Lulu Parcell?"

And oh yes—how in the world did you ever find such a thoughtful husband. Surely not in the Observer Want Ads! No matter how—I'm just the happiest person in the world—even considering!

Sincerely,

Frances Parcell

(letter #152)

Frances returned to McBee and to her adoring but mischievous students, while Bruce continued his work at Morris Field in Charlotte. On May 10 Frances wrote that she had arrived in McBee safely. Four of her students welcomed her. All of them were covered head to foot in a poison ivy rash. One of them was D.B., the boy who must have had a serious crush on his teacher. Before she left for the wedding, he had pleaded with her not to get married. As a last ditch effort to make her stay, he and some friends had gathered poison ivy and dumped it on her desk. His idea was that she would develop a terrible rash, get sick, and cancel the wedding. She did, in fact, get a bad rash on her arms, which she had to wrap in gauze underneath her wedding dress sleeves. D.B. did not know that not even fire and brimstone would have prevented the wedding.

Here is a short sampling of what they wrote while Frances finished up her obligations in McBee.

Monday night (May 11, 1942 postmark May 12)

Hello darling,

I've been accused of being in a dream ever since I came back. Can you imagine? I suppose I must look fairly dazed though because I've done nothing but wonder about you and what you are doing and hoping that you're having a terrible time without me. That's very selfish—see what a thing you're married to?

Of all times for me to come back to school this is the worst. Gas rationing begins tomorrow from four 'till nine and we won't finish up until Friday. Don't you forget to go register sometime. Doc says he doesn't see why you fellows don't get gas since you're working for Uncle Sam.

I didn't accomplish one thing today in school. The kids have asked me a million and one questions. D.B. wanted to know if it made me feel any different to be married—that put me on the spot. Do you feel any different, Lieut?

(from letter #156)

Just a little over a week after the wedding, Bruce wrote with some good news about a promotion.

Tuesday Night (May 12, 1942 postmark May 12)

My darling,

Today there came in the mail to one Lt. Parcel the next best letter ever—you're full of surprises aren't you? I am about the happiest –and luckiest guy I know right now. Somehow I have a guilty conscience for having so much more than other people—for being so fortunate when so many others aren't. It may sound strange but I do feel that way.

Lu, you aren't the only one who can have surprises. I have one for you. An extra good one too. I'd like to wait until you come on Friday but I know you would put me in the dog house so I suppose I'd better not. You see something new has been added! Darling, your husband is now a captain in the Army of the United States. Can you imagine that? The letter came this afternoon and I didn't waste any time taking my oath of office. It is effective from last Sat., so that is a very nice wedding present from Uncle Sam, don't you think? It was quite a surprise to me for I really didn't expect it for a while. Harry got his, too. The Post Exchange did a rushing business on silver bars this afternoon.

How is school? Time is passing so slowly now and I know it's weeks until you come back. Can't you burn down the school house or something?

I love you for always,

Bruce

(from letter #157)

The same day Frances wrote more about gas rationing. Apparently school teachers in her area were given the responsibility of issuing the ration coupons:

Tuesday (May 12, 1942 postmark May 13)

My dearest,

Since I'm writing everyone else I may as well write to you too—nice excuse. I've been writing letters and thank-you notes all afternoon. By some stroke of luck we only have to ration gas on Thursday so I've been free all afternoon. This rationing is certainly a pain—I don't understand all I know about it and from all reports the school teachers are going to get their necks broken sooner or later with this authority they're dishing out.

(from letter #158)

After the wedding they were initially only able to be together on weekends. It is not clear when Frances left McBee for good, but the last letter from May is postmarked May 20, so she probably moved soon after that. They only lived in Charlotte for a short time, and then they lived, in quick succession, in Myrtle Beach, South Carolina; Clearwater, Florida; and Sarasota, Florida, before moving to Walterboro, South Carolina, where the 405th Fighter Group was formed in preparation for service overseas. The Group consisted of three squadrons, the 509th, 510th, and 511th. Bruce was named commander of the 510th Fighter Squadron in November, 1943, in Walterboro.

At home in Charlotte, their first residence after their marriage

One of the rare stories that Mother used to tell about her early married life was about the bed bugs that had infested their first apartment in Myrtle Beach. The place was small and was named "Wee Scott." The bugs were so bad that the entire place had to be fumigated. In letters home to her parents she described the overwhelming insecticide fumes they had to deal with upon moving in.

There is not much information about their life as a military couple for a while. The next letters were written during a trip Frances made in January of 1943. She went to Barium, then to Thomson, Georgia, for a wedding. Anne Branan's sister Dot was getting married. About this time she began using Poppy or Pop as a pet name for Bruce. There is no explanation of why in any letter.

Friday morning (January 22, 1943 postmark Jan. 23)

Hello Mr. Poppy—

How does it feel to be a bachelor again? Don't repeat this but I shall never never want to be a spinster again for the plain and honest fact that I need to be protected—and anyway it's much more fun being married—to you.

Not having an alarm or telephone in our hotel room we slept until nine-thirty Thursday and our "early" start was a wee bit late. We got to Spartanburg around seven-thirty and I got a bus from there at eight-thirty but didn't get home until three this morning. Mom and Dad were waiting up for me with a pot of coffee and hot rolls. *(My grandmother's rolls were legendary)* Surely did hit the spot. It took me about as long to get from Spartanburg to Barium as it did to come all the way from Clearwater.

I'm sitting in Dad's easy chair before a beautiful fire—and getting so homesick for you I don't know what to do. It's very disappointing to move over in bed so Bruce can keep me warm and there's no Bruce. A hot water bottle has taken your place but it's not half as efficient because it gets awfully cold in the night.

Be a good boy and I'll bring you a surprise. I love you--------that much.

Yours only,

Lu

(from letter #163)

On the same Saturday night that Frances was relaxing in Barium in front of the fire, Bruce was in Florida feeling jealous because she was about to go to Georgia. He never could get over his feelings about the summer she spent in Atlanta with Charlie.

Saturday night (January 23, 1943 postmark Jan. 27)

Dearest Lu,

Tonight I am in one of my blue moods—if you know what I mean. Your letter came today, and it made me feel better, but right now I'm lonely.

I'm not a very good house keeper. Have spent 3 lonesome periods at the breakfast table and now in the kitchen there are 3 dirty bowls, 3 glasses, and 3 spoons. But maybe I'll get around to washing them before you get back.

Of course, sitting here by myself, I begin to get a little jealous—with you just before going to Georgia. Perhaps I'm a silly old fool, but I guess I love you so much I can't help feeling that way. This reminds me of Oakland—when I used to sit by the hour trying to write to you.

Lu, I miss you something awful. I love you, darling, and old fool or not, I think I can still tell you so.

Please be sweet, but careful, and watch out for the "Regiment" and Atlanta, etc. I'm just mean enough to hope you miss me an awful lot. Let me know when to expect you.

I love you

Bruce

(from letter #165)

Frances's letter that follows contains a reference to Bruce's niece and nephew, Sally and Bill ("the baby"), who was then called Little William after his father. They were the children of Bruce's sister Katherine. The family lived in Cleveland, North Carolina, where Mama Kate was originally from. Mama Kate often stayed with them as she had no real home of her own.

Wednesday night (January 27, 1943 postmark Jan. 28)

My dearest,

You're just the sweetest one! I was so blue because you hadn't written me and I tried very hard to know that you don't have time and hadn't really forgotten me—then a letter and a call all at once has made me quite happy again. As the days go by I'm all the more sure that I'll never, never leave you again—why it doesn't seem possible that I could miss you so much. I went over to Cleveland on the bus and Dad met me this afternoon at the station with your letter. Everyone was fine over there but they said it would certainly be nice to hear from you. The baby will be a year old tomorrow—he is still as "sweet as honey" and much cuter—I would like to take him home, but Sally was definitely opposed.

I can't wait to get home—(never to leave again.) Be sweet—I'll wire you what time I'll arrive. I love you, I love you. I love you.

Yours always-

Lu

(from letter #167)

A letter to her parents in March of 1943 gave Frances a chance to share a little of what her day-to-day life as an army wife was like. The wisdom tooth problem that she describes was a story she told often. My recollection is that she had to have it pulled and that resulted in a "dry socket" which was extremely painful. Memories of that tooth had not faded many decades later.

March 25. Thurs. (Postmark March 27, 1943)

Dearest Mother and Dad,

As of the 1st of April Bruce will be in charge of the squadron. He says he's pretty sure we'll be here another six months if not longer so we're looking for a place over on the beach but I doubt if we can find one because everything is so full. I hope Bruce will get some leave this summer but it's rather doubtful—he hasn't had but one day off since he had his cold and that surely is hard on him when his hours are so long. They had night flying last night.

Frances in Florida

I've been having trouble with my wisdom tooth again—it makes me hurt all over. I can't get an appointment with the dentist until next week but this is one time I surely don't mind going—and I don't think I'm any the wiser for the old tooth either!

We are sure having a tough time trying to find something to eat. The fresh vegetables are limited to carrots and cabbage, and potatoes are getting scarce—and of course there's hardly ever any meat or butter. We make a meal of course but it's rather monotonous. I'm not complaining though—it could be worse.

You should see my kitchen now—I painted the sink black and the drain a firehouse red. Bruce said I did that so the glare would wake him up when he got up to light the heater and heat my water. It just about has that effect once he gets in there, but I surely do have troubles getting him in there. Even with going to bed at nine-thirty we both feel like we haven't had enough sleep.

Did you ever have my pictures made? Put a note in your next letter so I'll know. Still haven't told Bruce. Looks like it will have to be an anniversary present. Only one more month and we'll have been married a year. Seems like a month. Take care of yourself and write us soon.

Love—

Lu

(from letter #168)

The letter also makes clear one of the problems of wartime life on the home front. Food shortages were common and many items such as cereal, processed and frozen foods, sugar, butter, meat, and coffee were rationed. In order to shop for groceries, it was necessary to present your government issued ration book containing the appropriate stamps.

The next separation came in October of 1943. Frances went home to be with her parents following the death of her brother Fred.

He was killed during a battle with the Japanese on July 30, 1943, in the South Pacific, but the family did not receive the dreaded "Killed in action" telegram until October 2. Up until then, he was officially listed as missing. Frances was devastated because she and Fred had

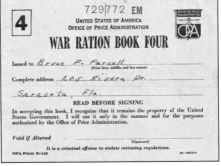

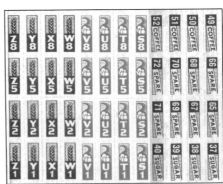

Ration book cover and ration stamps from 1943 when Bruce and Frances were living in Florida.

been very close. They were in the same high school graduating class because Fred had been held back a year somewhere during his school career. She was away from Florida for about a week and a half, returning after Fred's memorial service. As for the Civil War letter she mentions, it must have been lost over time. While doing some genealogy research, I discovered that Grandfather McNeely's father, the author of the letter and my great-great grandfather, was killed in the war in Petersburg, Virginia, in 1865.

One other fact that can be gleaned from this letter is that the envelope is addressed to "Major Parcell." In January of 1943 he was still a Captain. Some letters addressed to him from another family member indicate that by April, 1943, he had received a promotion to Major. This letter confirms that promotion.

Frances's brother, Fred Lowrance

Sunday (October 24, 1943 postmark Oct. 25)

Hello Poppy. I've been thinking about you all day. If I weren't so busy keeping Mom busy I'd be pretty sad. I am anyway 'cause I miss you so much. I know you're saying it was my own idea to come but it really was the best thing to do. Dad had written Wilson *(Skinny, her other brother)* saying he wished I could come but he would not ask me to leave you. So I guess things just work out for the best.

Grandfather McNeely *(Frances's maternal grandfather)* came up on the bus this morning before any of us got up. He's 81 and travels around like he was 18 instead. He had found an old letter written by his father to his grandmother in 1864 and he just had to bring it up to show Mom and Dad. His father was in Petersburg during the Civil War and he was telling about a certain attack they were making on the Yankees etc. It was rather faded but still readable.

Mother's flowers are so pretty. I picked enough for three bouquets this morning. They smell so good. She's saving the big ones for next Sun. Mr. Cook is going to have the memorial service for Fred then.

We are going to have Mrs. Gillespie come up for a while if she can. She is the wife of Fred's company commander who was killed. She may stay here a while after I leave. I hope so. It would help Mother as well as be a change for herself.

I love you best,

Mrs. P.

(letter #172)

Frances with her parents and Grandfather McNeely, whose father was a Confederate soldier killed in the Civil War in 1865. They are sitting on the front steps of the Lowrance home in Barium Springs.

Monday (October 25, 1943 postmark Oct 25)

My sweet Mr. Poppy—I'm just as thrilled about getting your long letter this morning as I was before we were married. That was such a wonderful letter and I guess I love you a thousand times better for such a masterpiece! I slept until ten thirty this morning but if I'd known your letter was here I'd have been up with the chickens.

Mother went to town this morning to get some curtain material for the dining room and bedrooms. She is getting a little excited about having Mrs. Gillespie come. Hope she can come now, so Mother won't be disappointed. We hope she'll come a week from today and stay after I'm gone. Hon, I think I'd better stay this week and part of the next anyway. I miss you something awful but I just feel that Mother will get over this so much faster if some of us are here. Guess you'll have to get a blonde companion to come stay with you. (If you do I'll kill you!)

(from letter #173)

Tuesday Night (October 26, 1943 postmark Oct. 27)

Hello Sweet,

Lu, I'm glad you went home, for I know it is a comfort to the folks. Maybe I'm selfish but I sure do want
you to come back. I'm beginning to lose all interest
in working or anything else. Can't even study my bridge
lessons. In other words, I am just plain lonesome. Perhaps you have
been too good to me and I am spoiled. Anyhow I won't be the same
again until you get back. It seems like an awful long time since you left.
So you bear that in mind and tell me when you plan to start back so I'll
have something to look forward to. Hear?

Give my love to Mom and Dad. And you stay sweet. I love you, Mrs. P.
I mean really.

Always,

Bruce

(from letter #174)

Wednesday (October 27, 1943 postmark Oct 27)

My dearest 'ole husband—

I'm right in the middle of answering more letters, memorials, etc. but
I knew you'd be getting madder and madder at me if I didn't write
again today. Mom and I spent most of yesterday in the antique shops—
just looking, pop-but it was fun looking anyway.

We had been in bed about an hour when you called the other night. I
wasn't asleep though. I'd been lying there thinking how nice it would
be to have you to snuggle up to and keep me warm, and how much
I miss you. Just before the phone rang I had to get up and examine
my bed—there was something in it, I just know, because every time
I'd get real quiet there would be a scurrying and scratching noise, but
I couldn't find the mouse or whatever it was. Anyway when I hurried
down to answer the phone I came minus shoes, and when some baby
mice on the other side of the room started squeaking I wanted to
take time out and get on a chair. I'm not afraid—I just don't like things
crawling on me. At any rate I sleep in the other room now—imagination or not!

We went up town this morning to get some pictures put in Mom's old
frames and to see about the antiques. Mother wanted them finished

before Mrs. Gillespie came but he won't get them ready I know. She's making me a dress this afternoon. Bruce—I know you're going to think I ought to come home sooner but honestly I don't know what to do. Mother needs me here, although she would say not to stay if I didn't want to. I love you and I miss you so much, and I want to be home with you, yet I feel like I should stay a little longer here. Please don't be mad with me 'cause I'm so lonesome and I love you more than anything or anybody.

If you're' a sweet boy and behave while I'm away I'll bring you two surprises instead of one.

All my love and a big hug and kiss,

Lu

(from letter #175)

Friday afternoon (October 29, 1943 postmark Oct. 29)

My dearest Bruce,

You spoiled me! I was expecting a letter today and didn't get one. I'm getting so homesick for my poppy.

I'm kinda blue this afternoon. Seems like I try to convince Mother that we have to take things as they come and for the best, but right now I feel like what's the use. Sometimes I don't think I believe in God or anything. That's wrong I know and I'm just selfish and self-pitying. Wish you were here to bring a little cheer.

Darling I promised a long letter today but like you I'm just filling up space. The only thing I can think about is that I miss you an awful lot and I want you so much. If I don't stop I'll be spilling tears. Write me a sassy letter, poppy.

I love you just heaps.

Lu

(from letter #177

DEPLOYMENT

Frances returned to Florida so no more letters exchanged hands until the next year rolled around. On November 5, 1943, they moved to Walterboro, South Carolina, where the men spent three months training for deployment overseas. As the war continued to drag on into 1944, plans for an allied invasion of the European mainland were underway. Bruce's 405th Fighter Group, part of the Ninth Air Force, was to play a major role in the build-up to the historic invasion. The 510th Fighter Squadron, under Bruce's command, flew operational exercises with the Atlantic Fleet out of their base in Walterboro. The pilots were gaining experience by flying P-39's and P-47's. They did intensive flight training for combat take-offs and landings, combat formation flying, aerial and ground gunnery, and aerobatics. The work was relentless and several pilot deaths resulted. Clearly the Army intended for its pilots to be combat ready when they shipped out.

Sketches by Frances during their short time in Walterboro

In Walterboro married men lived with their families in LaFayette Manor next to the Lady LaFayette Hotel.

Frances made friends with some of the other wives, including Cile Delashaw who was married to Bob Delashaw, the man who would one day become the

AMERICA'S MOST UNIQUE HOTEL   WALTERBORO, SOUTH CAROLINA

LADY LAFAYETTE TOURIST COTTAGES

commander of the 405th Fighter Group. This letter from Bruce to his in-laws displayed his usual reluctance to say anything negative about his current situation or his anticipated deployment. He was pretty vague about what was going to happen soon.

Walterboro, S.C., Feb. 6, 1944

Dear Mom and Dad,

There is a rather special reason why I am writing. I expect to be transferred pretty soon now, and I won't be seeing you for a while. I don't know where or when, but will let you know as soon as possible. I have been expecting it for some time, but under the circumstances and since I didn't really know for sure, I decided not to mention it. However, I am pretty enthusiastic about it and am satisfied that it will be O.K. So don't worry about it, I have not let Frances worry and I don't think she has very much. She will be able to tell you more about this later on.

Perhaps I will call you Tuesday or Wednesday evening. But don't worry if I don't for sometimes it is very hard to get a long distance call through.

Lu sends her love, and says she will write.

Love,

Bruce

(from letter #179)

9th Air Force 405th Fighter 510th Fighter
              Group   Squadron

The 510th Fighter Squadron that Bruce commanded, shown in Walterboro, S.C. shortly before they were deployed to Christchurch, England. Bruce is in the center, in the front row. Ralph Jenkins, who would succeed him as Squadron Commander, is on the far right, standing in the third row from the front.

Around this time, Frances went to the doctor at the military base because she was not feeling well. She was having nausea, which the doctors there diagnosed as possible ptomaine poisoning. Then she wrote a letter to Bruce while they were still together in Walterboro, in preparation for how it would be once he left.

Saturday (no date, no envelope, probably the morning of February 12, 1944)

Dearest Parcell,

Surprise! I'm waiting for you to come back from the field so I thought this would be a good time for me to start my letter writing.

I just wanted you to know that I've never been so happy in all my life as I have these past two years, and I want you to do a hurry-up job and get your fifty missions over so you can come back.

I'll be awfully lonely but I'll remember what you told me, and besides I guess maybe you'll be lonely too—I hope—anyway you keep up my morale with letters and I'll do likewise. I hear you coming so I'll close before you catch me—

Departure Day, February 12, 1944   *Frances in her loaded car, preparing to leave Walterboro for home at Barium Springs.*

All my love—

Mrs. P.

P.S. You're the best husband a girl could ever have!)

(from letter #180)

Bruce's letter here indicated that the Squadron's orders for departure must have come abruptly. Frances had already re-located to her parents' home in Barium Springs. The reference to the "loaded car" must have been to her sudden departure from Walterboro with a lot of their personal belongings. She left at noon on Saturday, February 12, a fact revealed in a later letter from Bruce when he was overseas.

Bruce departed from Walterboro two days later, on February 14, Valentine's Day.

Monday A.M. (February 14, 1944 postmark
Feb. 14, Walterboro, S.C.)

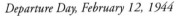

Dearest Lu,

Your letter surprised me, but it was the best surprise I ever had—I mean really! Your telegram came Sunday morning and I was relieved somewhat, for the car was loaded quite heavy.

Darling, I don't have much time, and things are happening all around me. Everyone is hustling around, so it isn't exactly a proper setting for a letter. However, I do want to let you know that everything is fine and we are all in high spirits—except for the fact that I miss you terribly.

What you said goes double for me, Lu. I love you, sweet, and will, always.

Please take care of yourself for me.

My love to everyone, and tell them how sorry I was that I wasn't with you. I will write as soon as possible.

Always,

Bruce

(letter #181)

He left by troop train on February 14, 1944, for Camp Shanks, New York. This huge facility was located thirty miles up the Hudson River from New York City. Camp Shanks was also known as "Last Stop, U.S.A.," because it was the largest point of embarkation for soldiers headed to the European front lines, including those who would be taking part in the D-Day invasion. It contained 1,500 barracks, heated by coal-fired, pot-bellied stoves. Roughly 1.3 million men and women received combat equipment and had final inspections there. Ominously, one of the pieces of equipment they were issued was a gas mask. The expectation was that the Germans would use chemical warfare as they had in World War I. As Bruce was absorbing the fact that he was far from home and would soon be in the war, he received this letter.

Friday, Feb 18 (postmark February 18, 1944 Emory University)

Dearest,

It seems like a short span from N.C. to Georgia but I thought we would never get here yesterday. I went to Charlotte with Mother and Dad and met Anne and Dot at the station. 'Course we rode in the coach and of course I sat behind a sailor with a box of cigars. Jim *(Jim Winslow, Anne's husband)* and his mother met us at the terminal.

Anne's house is adorable. She and Jim remind me of a couple of kids playing house—it really is a doll house. Being the artist, Anne has all manner of hanging plates and pictures. I can't say it measures up to our little beach apartment. Surely would like to know how you're making out but I know you won't be able to write. Did you have a chance to get your ring engraved? Don't forget what you're to have put inside.

My allotment hasn't come in yet and Gus says sometimes the ones they've gotten have taken eleven months to come thru. Either I live off my folks or go to work immediately. I'm not really worried though.

Don't get into too much trouble! I'm being awful good—just in case you're wondering—you so-and so-

I love you,

Lu

(from letter #183)

This did not sit at all well with Major Parcell.

Monday Night (February 21, 1944 postmark Feb. 26 New York City)

Dearest Lu,

You can see that your old man is getting in the groove with all this fancy letter writing. About Wed. or Thursday you almost weren't scheduled to get a letter, because tonight I almost didn't write one. That is because today I got your letter from "*Emory University*." That is some place in "*Georgia*," isn't it? Well, I was sorely disappointed because I had planned to call you this evening and then to discover that I couldn't—it was quite a blow. My morale is down quite a few points at this point. And I didn't tell you that I couldn't write to you!! Now I am at a loss as to what to do. Lu, I really didn't expect you to go down there until later. I have absolutely no right to be sorry that you went for I know you must be having a wonderful time. But you know me. Now I'd better shut my big mouth before I say something I don't really mean.

Don't worry about the allotment, Lu. I'll see that it is straightened out right away. Hardcastle has one that has already started, and he says it is late too.

I still have a slight cold and sore throat. Evidently the weather isn't agreeing with me—or me with it. So I'm staying in out of it. The only reason I didn't try to call you last night was because I was hoarse and was afraid that you might think I was sick.

Just stopped to read your letter again. Lu, you don't know how blue I am. I love you so very, very much. And I don't like the way you talk. You make me feel a though I had deserted you. Of course you won't have to go to work immediately as you say.

Darling, I'm going to stop now. Am all upset and will write again later. Just don't ever forget that I love you,

Bruce

(from letter #185)

He was on his way to war, and Frances was gallivanting off to Georgia, where she had met Charlie and had such good times with Anne and Jim. This letter, and others to follow, reflected how truly miserable he must have felt about leaving. Frances was missing him but had a cadre of friends and social events to keep her occupied. He was facing dangerous flights over enemy territory. He even wrote this to his in-laws.

Feb. 22, 1944 (postmark Feb. 25, 1944 NYC)

Dear Mom and Dad,

Please forgive me for not writing. It's been all I could do to write to Lu. I was so disappointed when I got her letter from Atlanta that I didn't know what to do. You see I had planned to call her that night. Of course she didn't know.

How are you? Please write to me real soon and tell me all the news. I was terribly sorry that I didn't get to see you both.

I've been having a very nice time. Have seen New York City and of course enjoyed that, having seen it only once before. Sure wish Frances was with me. Please look after her and don't let her get blue. I love her so very much and I want her to be happy.

Today it has been raining and as I have a slight cold, I have stayed in. Also, I have a good doctor to look after me and make me keep well in spite of myself. So don't you worry about me. I'll take good care of myself.

My best to everyone, and I miss you. Give Frances my very best spanking when she comes home. Don't let her stay in Ga!!

Love,

Bruce

(letter #189)

He really resented that Georgia connection and maybe justifiably so. Frances wrote him back, talking about how she was "so happy inside." This probably had to do with her visit to her doctor on February 16, once she got home to Barium Springs. She was still being bothered by that "ptomaine poisoning," which turned out to be morning sickness. She was expecting a baby *(me)* but she did not tell Bruce, not even when she spoke with him on the telephone when he called from New York. Later letters about this omission created much drama. She loved to tell that ptomaine poisoning story.

Wednesday, Feb. 23 (postmark date unreadable, Emory University)

Darling,

If I had you here with me I'd shake you good for being unhappy because I'm in Atlanta! You know there could never be anyone else but you—'ole doubting Thomas! I'm having as good a time here as I'll have at any place while you're away. The whole point being that I miss you so much that nothing interests me whatever and I sometimes have to pretend to be enthusiastic when I feel no such thing. So you see? Why should you worry?

Bruce, I'm just so happy inside that I can't tell you how I feel and what I want to say. Everything just adds up to I love you and I miss all your crazy capers and teasing and even your serious stern moods.

I'm not worrying about you Bruce as long as I know you're well and happy. It's wonderful that you're kept so busy.

Anne refuses to hear of me leaving before next Mon. So since I probably won't get back *(to Atlanta)* until next fall, if then—I guess I'll stay. It helps keep me occupied and my mind adjusted to being without you too.

I'll send Sarah the money and write everybody so you needn't to worry. I hadn't meant to give you the impression I needed the money from my allotment. I don't and probably won't any time soon. Clothes don't interest me even! I'm saving my clothes spree until Major P. comes sailing home.

I guess I could write all night about how much I love you but guess I better not. Don't worry and take care of yourself.

Yours always,

Lu

(from letter #190)

Now came an explanation for Bruce's being so upset about her trip to Georgia. The drama described here sounds like something made up for a Hollywood movie.

Feb. 24, 1944 (Postmark unreadable, New York City)

Hello darling,

Aren't you proud of me? Two phone calls. You don't know how much it meant to me to talk to you again. People around here can't understand the change in me. No foolin'.

Lu, I really am feeling a hundred percent better. It was, you might say, reassuring to talk to you. And sweetheart, I hope you didn't get the wrong idea from what I said. I was mostly teasing you, and at the same time trying to tell you that I don't exactly trust a certain other person. Now, I promised to tell you why. It's a long story—one I meant to tell you before now. But I didn't want to talk about anything unpleasant our last days together there. Also, I wasn't sure how you would react.

In the first place, it was entirely an accident and I stuck my big nose into something that was none of my business. You remember about two or three months ago when I "relapsed" into one of my moods. The last time that I acted so peculiar and you couldn't figure out why. Well, that day one of your letters to Fred came back. *(Letters to deceased servicemen were eventually returned to sender.)* It came to the field, and when I picked it up my first thought was to destroy it and save you the heartache I knew it would cause. Well, I opened it and glanced through it. It was a letter you had written just after coming back from Anne's wedding and in which you told him about seeing Charlie, and what he said to you. Lu, you know what reaction that had. It was all my fault and I felt terrible about it but it was too late. I'd already seen it. I couldn't tell you then but I had intended to later. Then, after it was all over, I forgot the whole thing. Except that you can see that I figured he still cared—and I definitely didn't like that. Then the fact that you had never told me anything about it, hurt me a little too. I always tried not to question you about it because I figured I had no right to do that. So I suffered in silence, so to speak. And darling, you don't know how badly I felt at times. That was the only reason I ever resented Anne or Jim. It would have been so much better if you had not tried to avoid the subject. I felt as though you didn't trust me.

Lu, you may still think all this seems foolish—even childish. If you could only realize that to me you are the most important thing in life—if you only knew how much I've always loved you—you might be able to understand that I couldn't help being jealous. It's a man's nature I suppose—and a weakness too.

At any rate, that's the whole story and if you want to never mention it again, why O.K. It isn't pleasant.

Guess what? I've received the notice of the allotment. It will go through OK now and you won't have to worry any more about it. The first payment should be before March 15th. I had just called over there *(to Newark, N.J.)* about it when I talked to you about it yesterday. That was one reason I was able to call you.

Lu, I've only received two of your letters so far. I suppose they will catch up sometime. It's sure bad not to hear. I'm just as unhappy about not hearing from you as I was two years ago. Darling, I'll always remember what you said just before we were married—about whether we would always be as happy as we were then. Well, I love you more than ever, and am about as happy as one person could ever be. Having you has meant more than anything else in my life, and without you, I would never have been able to carry on particularly over some of the rough spots. It hasn't always been easy for your and actually the past two years have been hard for you. You're about the best little soldier I've ever known and you deserve so very very much.

Darling, I haven't been drinking, and I am serious as ever I was in my whole life. I love you, Lu.

Goodnight.

Bruce

P.S. The censor should enjoy this!!!

(letter #191)

It took time for letters to make their way back and forth between New York and Atlanta, but Frances replied as soon as she heard of Bruce's concerns.

Feb. 28, 1944 Mon. (postmark Feb. 29 Atlanta)

My dearest,

This is one time I would fly to you if I just knew where I could get in touch with you. I received four of your letters today and the last one has just made me so unhappy. I can hardly stand it. The things I've called myself for making you unhappy—and so unnecessarily too—well I could say all the things—like I don't deserve such a considerate husband etc. and they would be true but I love you so much that I couldn't bear for you to believe them and perhaps stop loving me. I'll never in this world be able to put down on paper an explanation of my actions, but I'll try.

I'm sorry you had to discover whatever I said in Fred's letter because I hadn't meant to keep anything from you—it was just something that happened that meant nothing to me and I supposed that, feeling the way you did about my "Georgia past," that the less said the better. I merely mentioned it to Fred because he was always interested in the things I did and had known Charlie.

The night of the rehearsal party I was as natural with Charlie as I was with everyone else—simply because he didn't interest me in the least and I knew I had never loved and never would love anyone but you. To avoid what would have been quite a scene and to keep from putting a damper on Jim and Anne's party (because they've always treated me as their very closest friend and looked after my interests as much as their own) –well—Charlie took me back to the hotel, and en route became quite reminiscent and more than a trifle sorry for himself. Naturally I had never discussed you with him very much because I figured it was none of his business, but that night I set him straight in that I love you so much that nothing else mattered and it still goes. The times I had with Charlie were fun but not anything in comparison to just being with you. I realize more and more how foolish I was to have ever even thought I might have liked him at all. That year before you came back to N.C.—well—it was fun in an adolescent sort of way and I'd be crazy not to admit it, but I'm sure I'll make a better companion for having had my little experiences no matter how trite they seem now. The whole point is—what does it matter who cares about who as long as we love each other? I could bring up a few points in Parcell's "past" but the way I see it is that everyone is entitled to a few memories—good or bad—and I personally would rather know you as you are and not as you used to be. That was my whole point in avoiding, as you say, the subject.

I doubt that I've done anything but get you confused. To me, nothing in life is in any way important except you and making you happy. Please know that my heart actually aches because I've been so stupid about something so trite. I wish you had told me in Walterboro so I could know now that you understand my childish ways and forgive me. I love you, Bruce, more than anything in life. Until I hear from you again I'll be a little unhappy but please tell me everything is alright and that you aren't blue or angry with me.

I didn't go with Anne to town so I could write you. She's going to buy my ticket home for tomorrow. This is the last paper I had, thus the writing on both sides. Can't understand why you haven't received my letters. The censor will have a tough time with this, I'm sure. What a boring life he must lead!

Yours always

Lu

(letter #198)

There is a big discrepancy in this next letter between the date on the inside of the letter (February 16) and the postmark on the envelope (March 3). It was written just before Frances went to Georgia. This most important announcement of my impending birth was late to begin with and the delayed mail situation made matters worse. It would become a matter of contention by mid-April when Bruce finally found out he was to be a father.

Feb. 16, 1944 (postmark March 3 Statesville)

Dear Major Parcell:

A matter of great importance has been brought to our attention and we are extremely sorry it couldn't have been settled while you were in the states.

It seems you left a special order with us to be delivered sometime following the duration and six months. Due to wartime restrictions we won't be able to guarantee the full specifications of your order, but much to our good fortune we have been able to fill your order sooner than we expected. In fact you might expect the delivery around September.

In which case you are not present to receive and pass upon the specifications which you set up, we will place your bill of goods in capable hands until you return to claim that which is rightfully yours.

It is with great pleasure that we extend this good news to you and we express sincere hope that you will be the first to welcome your offspring into this world.

Very sincerely yours,

Stork, Inc.

Feb. 16 - 1944

Dear Major Parcell:

A matter of great importance has been brought to our attention and we are extremely sorry it couldn't have been settled while you were in the states.

It seems you left a special order with us to be delivered sometime following the duration and six months. Due to wartime restrictions we won't be able to guarantee the full full specifications of your order, but much to our good fortune we have been able to fill your order sooner than we expected. In fact you might expect the delivery around September.

In which case you are not present to recieve and pass upon the specifications which you set up, we will place your bill of goods in capable hands until you return to claim that which is rightfully yours.

It is with great pleasure that we extend this good news to you and we express sincere hope that you will be the first to welcome your offspring into this world.

Very sincerely yours,
Stork Inc.

109

CHRISTCHURCH, ENGLAND

While the tardy stork letter was floating around trying to find Bruce, he was on his way to war. On February 27, 1944, the 405th Fighter Group began the trip from Camp Shanks across the Atlantic on the Cunard White Star liner *RMS Mauretania*. The ship had had a short career as the fourth largest luxury liner in the world before being commissioned by the British government for use in the war, along with the *Queen Elizabeth* and the *Queen Mary*. She served during most of the war as a troop transport.

Some of the men suffered from sea sickness on the voyage but over-all the trip was uneventful. They sailed most of the way unescorted despite the very real threat from German submarines. The ship docked in Liverpool, England, on March 6. The men were greeted by children begging for chewing gum and candy. Loaded down with gear, they boarded a blacked-out train for Christchurch, a small town on England's southern coast, near Bournemouth and the Isle of Wight. The Fighter Group's new station was called Advanced Landing Ground 416. The pasture where the runway was located had to be lengthened and flattened to make it suitable for use by P-47s. Nearby were a Horsa glider factory, a group of British Navy firefighters, and some Navy test pilots.

In Christchurch, England, with good friend and fellow pilot, Alexander (Sandy) Johnston

The specialty of the 510th became armed reconnaissance. Ralph Jenkins, later to be commander of the squadron, said, "Call it what you will, it involved dropping 500 pound bombs with a release point calculated to provide sufficient altitude for recovery from the dive and avoiding collision with the target. After bomb release we would strafe with the fire from our eight .50 caliber machine guns. These guns were harmonized for 250 yards, so again, the attack had to be pressed to the point of near collision for best effect."

Officers of the Fighter Group and squadron commanders had living quarters in Brue Homage, an English manor house dating back to the reign of King George III. (The house has since burned down.) This was where Bruce lived until the group moved on to France in the summer. Here are his first impressions of England.

Somewhere in England, March 6, 1944 (postmark March 9)

Dearest Lu,

I love you! That's all I can think of to start off with, but then I really mean it. Lu, you don't know how much I mean it.

Now that I'm writing, I'm at a loss as to what to say, or tell you. You must realize that censorship is strict and so I will not be able to reveal much. I will not commit myself as to whether I like England or not, but will try to give you a few of my impressions. In the first place, the people impress me as being very friendly, although reserved. They don't possess that quality of idle curiosity which we find at home. Consequently, one hesitates to ask an Englishman where he lives or what has does for a living, or any of the usual things you might ask a person just in the way of making conversation. Later, I'll speak more of these things.

As for the country, one finds everything neat and orderly. There is no wasted space. You can't drive and see the kind of scenery you find along our highways. There are no ditches filled with underbrush, no land not being used for some purpose. Fields are separated by hedgerows, or fences. Generally speaking, you find that houses in small villages appear small—almost miniature. In other things too, one notices that England never developed on a large scale as did we. Trains are very small. Box cars, which are called "goods wagons" are less than half the size of ours. Still when you consider that England itself is small the reason of these things is quite apparent.

I hope that it doesn't take too long for you to receive my letters, but do be patient when they don't come and I'll do likewise on yours. I miss you, sweetheart, and love you with all my heart.

Bruce

(from letter #204)

The March letters talked a lot about the weather, which was cold in England, and about the erratic, unreliable mail service. Sometimes days would go by, both in Christchurch and in North Carolina, with no mail, then many letters would arrive at once. This one must have melted Frances's heart.

Somewhere in England, March 15, 1944 (postmark March 15)

Dearest Lu,

Your letters are finally finding me—four today. Perhaps I should have saved some of them for days when none arrive. That I could not do! One letter was written in answer to my little "confession." Darling, we certainly seem to have our troubles. I should have realized that it was not a very good time to be bringing up something like that, but on the other hand I wanted you to see my side of the story.

Lu, I'm selfish and mean—at least about that I was—and jealous too— very much so. Not because of anything you ever said or did—but just because that is my nature. I could never control it. Never was it your fault. Please don't feel badly about it. Anyway, that has been a long time ago now, and as you say, is of no importance. I merely brought it up before to explain why I felt as I did. I didn't want you to think it was a matter of mistrust—the reason for my apparently foolish conduct when I learned you had gone down there *(to Georgia)* so soon. On the other hand, Lu, I didn't tell you how I felt about Charles or about Fred's letter just because I wanted you to tell me about it. You know I didn't. I didn't expect you to mention it and actually I was sorry that you must have thought it necessary. Sometimes I wonder why you put up with me, darling. If nothing else, sweetheart, perhaps you know now what a terribly jealous husband you have, and that he would rather you tell him these things. Your theory that I wouldn't like it, and would get mad is wrong, darling. And anyway, you never tried to see!!!

I hope you have received several letters since that one, since you said you wouldn't be happy until you discovered whether I were angry with you. Actually, Lu, I am always restraining myself when I write to you. This is from the depths of my heart. You see, I always feel that if I say what I want to, you might think I was being too sentimental or mushy or something. Then I have the censor to consider, for I'm a bit timid myself. Or, again, maybe I don't think that it is proper for one to be so foolishly in love with his wife after being married for two years.

Lu, as I sit here and write this and think of you—or whenever I think of you for that matter—my heart beats just a little faster. My whole life now is wrapped up in you. I think in terms of what you would do or what you would say. I enjoy things because I think that you would like them too. You are always very near to me. That is what I was trying to tell you the other night in my letter. I never knew that two could be as one—could be so close together always, even when separated this way.

Darling, you remember that I told you once that I used to tell Harry about you, and that you were the one I wanted to marry someday. That was when I was in California before I came back East. I never knew whether you believed that or not. It was back then that I began to realize that I wanted you to love me. Then that night in Charlotte—when you said that you were afraid because I made love to you. Even then you didn't think I loved you. Lu, I worship you, and I have ever since. How foolish I was! I sincerely believed I was doing the right thing then by waiting to ask you to marry me. However, I wasn't very sure of myself then. After coming back and seeing you later on, I still thought I was right. During that time, I spent some most unhappy hours. Not unhappy either, but I was torn between what I wanted and what I thought was best for us. Then that night at Harry's when I made you cry, I knew that I was wrong. It was then that I knew that my life without you as a part of it was incomplete—that I didn't want to go on without you—that actually I was incapable of leading a normal existence without you as a part of it. Darling, human emotions are very strong. Thank God, I listened to my heart rather than my head, for my reasoning was wrong. My life since than has been more than complete. Often, I feel that I am so undeserving. I thank God for you –for your life—for your goodness—more than anything in this world I want a child who will be like you—as good as you. You see, there is more in my feeling for you than the love of a man for a woman which might grow cold and die. That I feel now as never before. Your complete happiness is my only concern and I pray always that this conflict may soon be ended so that we and everyone may pursue a normal life again.

Darling, my faith in what we are doing, and in the future, depends on yours. I can suffer anything, knowing that you can, too. Please remember that. After you lost Fred, you said something in a letter which frightened me. Please, Lu, never, never, let your faith in God be shaken. Promise me.

Sweet, I didn't know that I could be so serious or write so much. I promise to be in a more slap happy mood next time but it seemed I had to tell you some of the things in my heart.

I love you, always,

Bruce

(letter # 211)

She wrote to him on March 18, wondering if he had received her "stork" letter.

Saturday, March 18 (postmark March 19)

Hello darling

You'll never know how very glad I was to get your first letter *(from over-seas)*. Hearing from you is something extra special in my life, and I do enjoy your ramblings. The more you tell me what you see and do, the nearer you'll seem. It's like reading a book. I have to dream up the proper setting for the story or I don't enjoy it at all. So if you'll just give me the general set-up I can pretend, at least, that you're not so far away.

You didn't say enough about yourself though, hon—what kind of quarters do you have? Did you by any chance get sea sick going over? (You probably think that's an insult) Is it so terribly cold like everyone said it would be? My, there are so many questions I'd like to ask but you probably wouldn't answer them anyway. When you reach the point of censorship where you can't say anything just let me know you're my "faithful" husband and still well and happy!

I hope you've received all of my letters by now. There's one especially I'm most anxious to get an answer to—written Feb. 16. I haven't mentioned it since then because I've been wondering what reaction will come forth. Hope you'll be pretty happy when you do get it.

(from letter #214)

On March 23 Frances had decided she could wait no longer to break the news that Bruce was to be a "family man." She still did not know what might have happened to her stork letter.

March 23, 1944 (postmark March 24)

Dearest Major P.—

Tis high time the mail situation began to clear up! I simply cannot wait any longer to know if you've received my extraordinary news—as of Feb. 16th! So sit down and relax—you are soon to become a family man—a father no less! September 27 to be exact—or so the record says! I didn't tell you sooner because I thought you'd worry (that is, before you left.) So now you see—you must get this business over with extra quick and hurry home. After all I'd hate for the wee one to be playing marbles –or maybe craps—before you return! Seriously darling—I think it's amazing and I can hardly believe it, but I'm terribly happy over the prospect. That certainly settles the working situation at any rate. Mom and Dad will hardly let me turn around by myself, let alone get a job! Dr. Shaw is taking awfully good care of me and I'm quite a healthy patient, so you need not worry about the care I'm getting. I'm awfully upset that you haven't heard from me though, and I hope you'll let me know just as soon as you do hear. I always did like to share good news, while it was still new. This calls for a celebration, but guess that can wait until you're here in person rather than in spirit!

The sooner I hear from you the sooner I'll settle down to normal living—hope you're as happy as I am.

I love you—more every day—and miss you more than that.

Yours always,

Lu

(letter #218)

Probably because of a March job assignment that Bruce received, he was getting letters only sporadically. He and Bob Delashaw traveled to the Anzio beach head on the west coast of Italy to observe and participate in dive bombing missions there. This was supposed to help them prepare for D-Day and its aftermath. They had to go by way of Algeria, but Frances knew nothing about his travels, all of which made for great confusion. He wrote from "Somewhere in North Africa" and "Somewhere in Italy." Enclosed in this letter was a clipping from the *Stars and Stripes*, Italian edition. It showed a picture of Mt. Vesuvius in full eruption, with a huge cloud above it. The text said it was the greatest eruption of the volcano since 1872.

Bob Delashaw, someday to be Bruce's commanding officer. He ended his military career as a general.

Somewhere in Italy, March 28, 1944 (postmark March 31,1944)

Dearest Lu,

Again I surprise you with a letter. You must be won-  dering what I am up to. Even if it were possible to say, I doubt if I could tell you. Suffice it to say that I am well and still doing fine. Your letters would certainly help a lot naturally. Still, I expect to receive them and then what a time I will have.

Perhaps you have read of the eruption of Mt. Vesuvius. It is near Naples and is visible from there. I have had the opportunity of visiting that city and will send you something which I purchased for you there.

Lu, it's awfully hard to write when you haven't received any mail, and when you have to be so careful of what you say. Perhaps later on I can tell you of some of my experiences.

Right now I sure do miss you. Letter writing doesn't always make me lonesome and blue, however. By now, spring should be just around the corner, and you should have been out shopping for a new Easter bonnet. Wish I could be helping you.

(from letter #225)

This was not especially helpful information. Another Italy letter followed.

Somewhere in Italy, April 2, 1944 (postmark April 4, 1944)

Hello Sweetheart,

There is almost a full moon outside and it sure does things to me. That is, it would if I were not in Italy, but were somewhere way down south of the Mason Dixon line, namely, in North Carolina. As it is, there is quite a lot of consolation in being able to write to you. Then too, I can remember other times and other moons, as well as look forward to other moons to come. I hope they won't be too far away, darling. The idea is that I love you more than anything. See?

Incidentally, Mrs. P, something funny just occurred to me which you will most likely approve of highly. It appears that in Italy a gentleman taking a lady out must be accompanied by her mother, brother or some member of the family. And I didn't find that out from experience. It was merely told to me! However, I understand that down in Africa a man can have four wives, and they do all the work! He sits around and plays dominoes all day and, well, I don't know about their night life, but most families have dozens of children!

That seems prevalent here, at any rate. There seem to be more children than grownups. They all stop you and ask for "chew" or "caramels." The other day I saw two little boys about three and five years old sitting by the road. I gave the oldest a stick of gum and his face lit up with a big smile. He unwrapped it and gave half to his little brother, so I gave them another stick. There is a little girl named Anna who lives nearby. She is five, and very cute except that the other day I caught her smoking a cigarette!

Good night, darling. It's late. I love you more and more as the days go by. Be sweet and remember I'm always happy if you continue to keep up my morale. I love you, Lu.

Bruce

(from letter #228)

About the same time Frances wrote this:

Monday, April 3, 1944 (postmark April 3, 1944)

Dearest Bruce

This mail system, as I've said so many times before, is certainly peculiar. I got your V-Mail yesterday after having received four letters. Evidently you haven't received my cable or any of my letters since you sent your address again. I'm as anxious as you are for my letters to reach you. You're probably feeling very neglected, but I have written and you know you're in my thoughts always.

Darling my curiosity is just about to get the best of me! This business of becoming a parent for the first time would be so much more thrilling if I knew you were sharing my happiness. When I'm not thinking of you and the crazy happy hours we had together, I'm dreaming of our coming offspring. At the moment a name, although there seems to be ample time for that, has me a little perplexed. I haven't quite put the child through college yet, but in my mind I've hatched up all sorts of ways to make "father "seem a reality until you do get back. Perhaps the War Department won't agree with me but I'm expecting you home before the wee one is over six months old. That is a hunch! Optimistic soul, aren't I?

(from letter #227)

By April 6 she was talking about "our blessed event," telling Bruce about her baby clothes purchases, assuming he must surely have received the news by then. In this next letter she indicated that she had finally received the long romantic one from him, written on March 15.

April 8, 1944 Sat.

Dearest Mr. Pop,

After all the wonderful letters I've been getting from you, I feel that I'm not quite capable of keeping up with you. There never was in this world such a wonder, and I might add a nicer husband, or a more romantic lover, or a more desirable companion than one B.F. Parcell!

I received three letters yesterday—one very, very special one—mailed in England. You know it's a good thing I don't have a job. I'd never in this world be able to keep my mind on my work, especially if you wrote many letters like the one I got yesterday. As it is, my daily existence revolves around "What Bruce did" and "What Bruce thinks" and "What Bruce would say if I did so and so."

It looks as if we're going to have a very cold and rainy Easter after all but come what may I'm wearing my purple hat, just for the sake of morale. Although you fixed that quite well with a letter yesterday. Bruce I can't tell you how happy you've made me, even if I am so undeserving of all your praise and love.

Honestly hon, I can't get you settled on one part of the map until you're elsewhere. Perhaps your frequent station changes will benefit my knowledge of geography as well as your own. I'm terribly sorry you aren't getting my letters. Yours are a constant source of joy to me. I don't get them every day but this past week I've been quite lucky, nice Easter present. Do tell me more about your "sightseeing."

There's so much I have to be thankful for. Being married to you most of all and having had two perfect years even with a few disagreements etc. We've already had so much more than most people have and when I think of the future, there's even more happiness to look forward to. Perhaps I sound a little optimistic, but my faith in you and in God give me the reason to be. We never discussed our beliefs or disbeliefs very much, maybe because we took our religion for granted. After Fred's death I did feel a little confused, but I promise you, Bruce, that I'll never lose faith again.

You mustn't worry about my morale darling. Besides having your letters, I now have a responsibility that requires a very high morale which is not hard to obtain, as you should know, remembering how much I've always wanted a child.

The whole thing adds up to the fact that I love you so much that I chatter on and on about nothing to keep from getting too sentimental. Please stay put long enough to get my letters. Take good care of yourself.

Yours always,

Lu

(from letter #234)

April 10, 1944 Monday (postmark April 10, 1944)

Hello my dear Major P. This is one glorious day, actually spring and what it hasn't done to my spirits! I've just been torturing myself by sitting out on the upstairs porch trying to regain my Florida tan. Can't notice any difference except that I've six million more freckles and am four times as hot as I was. Surely brings back memories of Clearwater. I closed my eyes and pretended I was on the beach but it was a little hard to make believe when the sea breeze was absent and the wasps insisted on using me as a part of their maneuvers. That at least never happened on the beach.

I remember a great deal about Florida, the beach, and you, but best I don't go into that. I write you all the silly insignificant things I do, simply because my life is quite uneventful without you. I never thought I'd depend on one person (especially Bruce Parcell who never ever showed me the slightest particle of attention) for my happiness, but I do and I even like it!

Mother is just beside herself when it comes to buying for the baby and me too for that matter. She gave me a white wool blanket and a precious pair of booties and a gown for myself for Easter. I feel like I'm collecting a trousseau again. A little difference in the style of the collections though.

(from letter #235)

Bruce's final letter from Italy arrived, full of touristy information.

Somewhere in Italy, April 9, 1944 Sun. (postmark April 10, 1944)

Dearest Lu,

We didn't have too nice a day for Easter. It rained a little this afternoon. However, I went to church this morning. The service was very good and in a lovely old church. I saved the bulletin and will send it to you later.

Lu, I've visited the ruins of Pompeii. Several of us found a guide who took us through. A most interesting fellow, himself. Pompeii, if you remember, is the city that was covered by ashes from an eruption of Vesuvius back in 79 AD and discovered in the sixteenth century. Excavation began in 1748 and has continued ever since. There is about 2/5 of the city still covered. The unexcavated part is now about 30 to 40 feet under ashes and dirt.

It is the most amazing thing I've seen in a long time. There is a wealth of information that has been learned about the civilization of that time, particularly of the Roman Period. Considering the riotous way of living that is apparent, the place must have been destroyed for its sins. However, there is much that was beautiful in the way of architecture, painting, and sculpture.

But I mustn't turn this into a history lesson. It is a little late, but I decided it was time to write to you again. Also, I had to remind you that I miss you very, very much, and love you even more. Darling, you are still with me every waking moment, and I am only sorry that I don't dream of you every night.

All my love,

Bruce

(letter #236)

Frances often rambled on about the daily details of life in Barium.

April 12, 1944 Wed.

Darling,

Dad has gone to prayer service and Mother is scraping away on some wood she intends to make a stool from. Honestly she can think of more things to dabble in. She has been after Mr. Irvin to make her a kitchen table with no results so she has made one herself, and the amazing thing is that it really looks like a table! Mother of course would have to have it as near like an antique as possible, so she put it together with wooden pegs and wouldn't use any kind of wood except knotty pine with worm holes! I dare not think what fad will be next.

I was all set to make your cookies yesterday and found we didn't have any sugar or butter. I promise to get them made very soon though. Mom and I've worked out a little system. I cook for three weeks then she takes over. Since my vacation of several months, I feel quite, quite green at this. I have to watch Dad out of the corner of one eye to see if he eats my fancy dishes because he likes them or is afraid he'll hurt my feelings.

I love you just lots and lots,

Mrs. P.

(from letter #237)

April 15, 1944 Saturday (postmark April 17, 1944)

My Dearest,

This has been one of my off weeks, maybe because I haven't had a hunch as I usually do about a letter. My fingers are crossed for tomorrow but the hope is faint. Maybe too I'm just now beginning to realize how far away you really are and how terribly long it will be before you're with me again. I scold myself every so often, because I know that the only way time and loneliness without you are going to go swiftly is when my mind is occupied with something very definite to do. Only sometimes especially at night I begin to dream of your homecoming and the many, many things we'll have to talk about and wondering how you'll look when you see our child for the first time and hearing you laugh again. I love your laugh because it seems to come from all of you, not just your lips, and teasing you again, and most of all I dream of just being able to be near you and talk to you again. Sometimes I think of you so hard I'm sure you must know. You're always in my thoughts. I cook the things you like. I wear the dresses you like, the records I play are your favorites. In other words you're always near me in a sense, but my whole heart won't be in anything I do until you're actually here to share with me.

(from letter #239)

At last, on April 16, Bruce wrote that he had received the letters about fatherhood. He was thrilled but also puzzled about why it took so long for him to find out.

Somewhere in England, April 16, 1944 Sunday (postmark April 17, 1944)

My darling,

Some time ago, before my trip, I wrote you a very long letter in which I told you of the things which were in my heart. At that time I had not received a certain letter which you were anxious to receive an answer from. Yesterday I returned with Bob from my trip *(to Italy)*. There was a lot of mail. This, then, is the answer you have been waiting for so long. It was a trick of fate that so much time has passed.

Lu, last night I sorted your letters in proper sequence. It was late, for all the fellows had been engaging me in a lengthy discussion of my late actions. I was over in Bob's room, where he had been reading his mail from home. He had a funny grin on his face! He knew!! What fun he had watching me open my letters. I finally came to the letter. I almost fell off the bed I was sitting on. Honest. That moment will always be held in my memory as one of the happiest in my life. My hand trembled. I was astounded. It was beyond comprehension, and I had to force myself to realize that it was true. Darling, to know that you will bear our child is for me the fulfillment of my most cherished hope. My love for you is without bounds. I am so overwhelmed that all words have fled my mind. Last night I thanked God for His goodness to me, for you. You have made my life complete.

Lu, all this and more, is my answer. I cannot conceal my feelings. If I am selfish, forgive me. Please tell me that you are glad I feel this way.

With my joy, there is also deep concern for you. My darling you are my life. You must take care of yourself. You must be happy too, or I, well, I could not find life worth living.

Now it is my solemn duty as a husband to scold you. Actually, young lady, if you were here this minute, you would receive a spanking like you never received before from me or anyone else! Why? Because you have been so utterly secretive about this to me. Both Bob and Sandy knew before I did. Still I am confused. You have got a lot of explaining to do. In a letter of Feb. 16, mailed at Barium you said that you were sending me a little surprise! On the 18th, you wrote from Anne's but no mention of the surprise. On the 24th of Feb. I talked to you on the telephone and you didn't tell me. That afternoon you wrote and said that you did have something good to tell me but you wouldn't tell me over the phone. You little d----!! How I yearn to spank you!!

Now, on March 1st, from Barium, you asked if I had gotten the little surprise yet. Quote "Should surprise you 'cause it did me." Unquote. At the bottom of this letter you promised to write a real special letter tomorrow," and it was postmarked March 2nd. On March 3rd you mailed two letters. One told me that you were mailing "that very special letter I promised" and that you expected a very special answer. Darling, the very special letter was mailed on the 3rd---but it bears a date inside, top right corner of Feb. 16, 1944!!!! Now, how can I ever find out these things, especially such a very, very,

very important thing, if you write on Feb. 16th and mail same letter on March 3rd?? On March 19th you asked if I had received that letter written of Feb. 16th, because you were anxious about my reaction.

Lu, were you afraid to tell me? Darling, that grieves me, if it's true. Didn't you know how I would feel? You must have. Please don't tell me you thought I would feel any other way. And when I talked to you, Lu, why I could--well I hereby solemnly promise that I will spank you across my knee for not telling me then. You little rascal. Then you say in a later letter that I might have received this news and ignored it. That will cost you a second spanking. I am in dead earnest.

Promise me that you will never, never do anything like that again. My sweetheart, I love you so that my heart aches. I could write all night. Already I've forgiven you but the one spanking still stands!

Your ever faithful husband,

Bruce

(letter #240)

Just in case, he also sent a telegram.

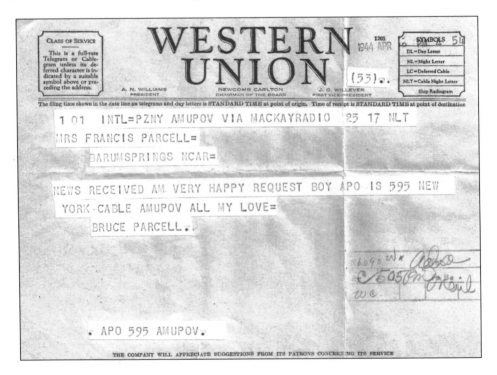

Then, the next day he wrote again.

Somewhere in England, April 19, 1944 Wed.

Hello, sweetheart,

Three letters from you today—one long one written on April 8th. They come in out of order though, and keep me quite confused most of the time. The letter of the 8th wasn't mailed until the 10th, so you can see that the situation is improving. As for Vmail, they don't come any faster, and of course I'd rather have longer letters, too.

Lu, your letter on Easter did sound just a little blue. That's ok. You keep telling me that you have so much to say, but don't quite write it down. And you tell me about letters you write and don't mail. Sweetheart, I want you to write to me just what you feel. Sometimes I can sense that you're trying to be light and gay when you aren't. Now you know me better than that, don't you? I feel you are leaving me out if you don't express yourself to me. Honest! And surely I don't expect you to be carefree always. Not when I'm not that way. If things seem to go wrong and you need me, just go ahead and write as if you were talking to me instead. Surely, I've tried to do that, and it works, too. Perhaps I am a little too sentimental at times, but I mean and feel every word I say, even more. You know what I think? I think you are a wee bit bashful. The idea of trying not to get sentimental! If you only knew how much I want you to! Actually, that's what keeps up my morale. All you have to do is say something extra sweet and I am in high spirits for days. Darling, I love you with my whole heart. I will always think you are the sweetest, and the nicest person on earth. Now don't be saying I shouldn't say things like that! I can remember once when you were afraid that I would become "indifferent" after we had been married for a while. Remember? Actually, I become more in love with my wife every day. Since you told me of the great news, I have been happy beyond description. I think of you every minute, Lu. It's all too good to be true, really. It was you who was skeptical, though. Darling, I suppose you know I want a son. If you don't agree or aren't willing to change your mind, that's ok by me. If you do though I have an idea I'll get my wish. Actually, by a strange coincidence, you got my reaction to this before I ever even realized. Remember I said in a letter that I wanted child, one who would be ours, and as good as you. I meant that then as well as now. My heart overflows every time I think of it which is all the time. Now, who is sentimental? You are the sweetest thing this side of heaven.

"Your ever faithful husband with warm feet,"

Bruce

(from letter #243)

Bruce's happy but scolding letter finally arrived at Barium. Here is the reply. These two had a lot of misunderstandings via the postal service.

April 23 Sunday (postmark April 24, 1944)

My dearest Bruce,

There are so many things I want to say that there doesn't seem to be a starting point. First off though, I want you to know I love you very, very much and your always perfect letters are so wonderful that I hardly feel that my few scratchy letters are worthy of your time!

Dear me, but it does seem as if I've gotten myself into terrible trouble! As you've always said, my logic never made sense, but in this particular instance I just knew I was right and maybe you'll see later why. With all your dates and what not you've gotten me a bit confused but anyway, my purpose in waiting to mail the letter of Feb. 16 until you had left New York, was that you might worry and I was certain you had enough to occupy your mind as it was. My "figuring" was that you'd surely get the letter among the first mail after you'd settled in one spot over there .You'll never know how much I wanted to tell you before and especially on the telephone (with ever so many people listening in). Bruce, please don't be angry with me. (I'll take the spanking though.) I thought my way was best, knowing how you do worry about me when I'm ailing. At any rate you'll only have five months to wait until you're a parent. It may not to you but it seems to me, with these first few months and five more, well it is just eternity!

I'm terribly sorry Bob *(Delashaw)* and Sandy *(Johnston)* found out before you did. At first I wasn't going to tell a soul until you knew, but somehow people always find out so then I wrote Cile and Frances *(wives of Bob and Sandy)*, warning them not to tell the boys until you had heard the glad tidings. Those two couldn't keep anything secret two minutes.

Darling I can't tell you how I felt that day, Feb. 16. You may have been a little astonished but I think poor Dr. Shaw thought my world had come to an end. As a rule I control my emotions fairly well in the presence of strangers but I was so terribly happy that I couldn't have kept back that flood of tears no matter how hard I tried. He has a nice big fatherly shoulder that I saturated quite well and he was the most relieved looking person when I finally told him how glad I was. You need never be concerned about my welfare while he and Mom are looking after me.

I feel that no one else in the whole world has had such an amazing thing happen, which is very foolish 'cause it happens every day. I think we're pretty special though, don't you? Hon, when you finally get used to the idea of becoming a father, how about giving me some ideas on names? The child does have to have a name, you know, and since it will be a very special child, the name should be very special too!

I do hope I've squared myself as to the delay in letting you know of our good fortune. I love you most in all the world.

For always,

Mrs. P.

(from letter #247)

Bruce's letter of April 24 mentioned their "relationship of old." It gives a tantalizing clue as to why that Thanksgiving rendezvous turned out as it did.

Somewhere in England, April 24, 1944 Monday (Postmark April 26, 1944)

Hello, Sweetheart,

It's good to hear that you are enjoying spring weather. As for the freckles, I love you twice as much for each one of them. I too, think of Florida and miss it and you, especially you. Someday I expect to make up for you all the long hours you used to spend waiting for me to come home. Always I feel that I owe you so much, darling. You missed an awful lot because of me but I could never have gotten along without you. Nor could I ever get along, or be happy without you from now on. And my dear young lady, I still contend that our relationship of old (when you say I paid no attention to you) was as much your fault as it was mine. If I hadn't finally "taken the bull by the horns" so to speak, well it frightens me to think of it.

So now I want you to tell me all about yourself, and our future. You don't mention it much at all. You haven't expressed any desire for a boy or girl. Darling, all the little, inmost thoughts are so important to me. What you have picked for a name and all that. Actually, I don't think I'll ever quite forgive you for not telling me before I left the States, nor will I understand why you thought it would worry me. I've been waiting for your reply to that! Lu, when did you first know? Or did you merely suspect it before I left?

I love you, sweet, and long to hold you close in my arms again.

Always,

Bruce

(from letter #251)

Notably absent from Bruce's letters was any information about what he was doing during his time in Christchurch. He could not say much because of the censor, and Frances must have been mostly in the dark about his activities. In fact the 405th Fighter group did sweeps, escorts, strafing, and dive bombing missions over German-occupied France all throughout April and May. They attacked trains and radio stations, among other targets. In this nice newsy letter, Bruce painted a picture of what life was like in England. Typically he made everything sound wonderful.

Somewhere in England, April 28, 1944 Friday (postmark April 30, 1944)

Hello Sweetheart,

Lu, I promised to tell you more of myself and the country.

You have some ideas about England from pictures, newsreels, and what you have read. Well, I found that those impressions are pretty accurate. Of course London is "the" metropolis and I have not seen that city. England is a small place though and apparently life and customs aren't as varied as, say between Florida and N.Y. or California.

Everything is in conformity with the small size of the country and its comparatively large population. Roads are narrow and all cars are small and economical. Of course driving is on the left side of the road. That is a very annoying custom. Then, everyone seems to have a bicycle. Even I am getting my exercise by riding one daily. The people, due to congestion I suppose, have an aloofness which must have been developed in order to preserve some privacy. Also, they have developed a deep respect of the rights of the individuals.

What I'm trying to say is that the average Englishman isn't chummy. He won't engage a stranger in conversation normally. Some people have misunderstood this attitude and attributed it to snobbishness. This isn't true at all and actually the people are very friendly when one gets to know them.

They have a great love for their country and a devotion to their tradition. Land is precious and looked after with great care. The countryside is beautiful, not in a rugged sense, but neat and orderly. Apparently it stays green, because of the predominately wet climate. (Incidentally, I find now that the sun does shine in England occasionally!)

However, England is behind us in so many things. Public health and sanitation is an example. Here you would buy your bread from a bread wagon unwrapped and handled by the seller. Milk is not pasteurized, nor are cattle always inoculated.

Telephone service is inferior to ours. I could mention many other things. We, at home, have come to consider luxuries as necessities. I am firmly convinced of that.

But to get to something closer to myself. Naturally I can't say where I am. However we aren't far from a town. One never is in England. The surrounding countryside is lovely. My quarters are in a building that was once a private home. It compares in size with Lee's Cottage *(a Barium dorm)*, and has lovely immediate surroundings. There is a beautiful huge rhododendron bush outside my window. It is now in full bloom and how I'd love to send you some of it!! There is also a lot of wisteria in bloom.

We have managed to make things quite comfortable. Yes, I even get a hot bath when I want it! We have a good mess, and even have an electric toaster on the table. Food is quite good, too.

You asked about things such as candy and cigarettes. We receive sufficient of these things. Reading material is a little old, but we have it and it's new to us. I'm speaking of American magazines. Our source of news is the radio and a daily paper, "The Stars and Stripes." Incidentally this contains "Terry and the Pirates," and "Little Abner." *(comic strips)* You know I could never get along without that! Then too we get the "Yank" weekly.

There are plenty of American movies and often new releases.

Darling, if I keep this up, you will begin to think that my life is too good, and wonder if I really do miss you and home. My answer to that is this: My sole desire now is to see the end of this war and to return to you. Nothing can or ever will lessen my desire to return to a normal way of life. Nothing can ever change my love for you. If anything, all this only adds to it, even as it has made me appreciate our own way of life and our own country. I thank God that we have been spared the suffering and misery of war at home. I don't mean that I have seen a lot of it in this country, but it exists wherever war has touched. If I can feel that I have done my share to stop it, I will be satisfied.

But enough of this. I'm interested in what you are doing and how you are. You must write regularly now or I will worry about you. How I regret that I can't be with you. Darling, you must exercise your every effort and will power to live a normal existence. You must not worry about me. I am unimportant now in your life as compared with the new life which will be our child.

Lu, you are ever a constant source of strength to me. I love, you darling, now and always.

Bruce

(from letter #253)

Frances wrote more about having a baby and also about how she thought about their past. It seems amazing, viewing this relationship in hindsight, that it took them so long to discover their love for each other.

Saturday, April 29 (postmark April 29, 1944)

Living without you is so much harder than I ever expected it to be, but when you write I can almost believe you're here and it's easier too when I know you're having a little fun along with your duties. It isn't any harder for me here at home, darling because Mom and Dad are so terribly good to me, as is everybody, and after so long a time, I'm beginning to "organize" my life in such a way that I'll "exist" until you get back to share everything with me. I especially try not to ever be blue, not only for your morale and mine but also for our child. Perhaps I should be very definite and determined and say son. You seem to have made up your mind and intend that mine should be the same. You know, they tell me that only God and nature can determine such matters, so don't you be disappointed, Bruce Parcell, if a girl arrives. It's a little soon for me to have a "hunch" but later on I'll make a bet with you as to the outcome though.

You know the very idea of having a child is almost as amazing as being married to you—that I'll never cease to wonder over. Not just because it's near our second anniversary, but I often think how fantastic it seems for you and I to be husband and wife, really seems like a dream that couldn't have come true but did. You would probably be even more amazed if you knew how I used to make up things about you so as to convince myself I didn't care for you. Bruce Parcell, you were the most indifferent somebody I ever did know, and I just decided I was wasting my time and eating my heart out over some fickle fellow who'd never give me a second thought. During the first few weeks after you came back east on maneuvers and later too, I'd get so furious with you that I determined never to see you again, but of course my resistance wasn't very good as you found out.

I really don't deserve these few years of complete happiness, before and after our marriage. Even though we're apart now I think we are really the luckiest people in the world. Our love and soon our child is enough to keep us close even though the miles are great between us.

Mother laughs at me (not seriously though) when I go shopping. I'm either buying something, material etc. to make the baby some clothes or else I'm getting something to make my "second" trousseau. You see, I intend to have that ten days' honeymoon the army promised us two years ago!

That reminds me, I want to decide on a name for the "little major" before he arrives so don't you forget to tell me what you like. Of course if it's a girl the name will be Anne something or other. I don't want to do this naming all by myself. Heed my words, sir!

Yours only always,

Lu

(from letter #254)

Frances sent this picture to Bruce sometime in the spring of 1944. On the back she wrote "Mama P." She is in the back yard of the Lowrance place in Barium Springs.

On May 2, they had been married two years. They reminisced about that and talked more about the baby to be. It does seem strange that they were certain that the baby would be a son. They hardly ever mentioned the possibility of a girl.

Bruce dearest,

Happy anniversary! My first thought this morning was, what a beautiful day for a wedding! And it has been such a very short while since May 2 two years ago. I guess you know I love you twice as much as I did then, and that's an awful lot. Trying to tell you exactly what's in my heart is just like moving a mountain. Perhaps I am a bit bashful when I write down the things I feel so strongly but you see, having never been very demonstrative as to my feelings (before you entered the picture), I can't seem to believe this is really me. You mention in most all your letters that I must write exactly what I think, and I feel a little distressed that I can't. Maybe if I only missed your companionship and love a little bit I might be able to say all that my heart holds but as it is, it's beyond my power to write in just simple words that without you, life holds no meaning. My arms feel so empty, to say nothing of the hurt feeling in my heart. I often think if just for one day I could have you close to me, hear you laugh and argue a little, even just be in the same room while you were reading or more than likely sleeping, or maybe sit beside you in a movie and have your hold my hand. I'm sure one day wouldn't be enough but it would help to break the loneliness I feel. You need never feel that you owe me anything, Bruce. The times I had to wait on you to come from work, well I might have seemed impatient and unhappy about waiting, but it was only because I begrudged the Army the time I could have spent with you. I know now it's best to live each day as if there would always be a tomorrow, whereas I always had in the back of my mind that you would leave someday, and I guess I was trying to store up a little extra living. I hardly see how two people could have been any happier, and you, my own sweet husband, were the cause of it all. Don't you dare say you want to make up to me all the things I've missed. Just having you for my very own is all I ask.

The one thing that really keeps my chin up is the knowledge that someday you will be home and although our lives will be a little different now, we can take up our happiness just where we left off. Another thing—your remarkable letters , so like you that I want to weep, always are reminding me that I can be as good a soldier as you and too the idea that we'll soon have a child all our own is more or less stimulating to the morale.

You said I never mentioned my plans for the future, but I was just thinking you might feel I was spending too much time with the future and ignoring the present! It's still a little hard for me to realize we're going to have a child and I know it must be for you. Although there is absolutely nothing to worry about, I sometimes get a little frightened at the idea of bearing our son alone. If anything should happen it would be my fault and I couldn't bear to have you love me any less, as is quite possible. Our hearts sometimes change when something so big and so wonderful is anticipated, then is lost. I'm not being pessimistic, darling, because I think it's only sensible to look at the dark side in this case as well as the bright. I pray each night that God will help me through this time and give us a healthy son in time. I know you understand how I feel. If you were by my side I wouldn't give it another thought. That's how terribly much I depend on you.

If I've hurt you by not telling you about a baby before you left, please, please forgive me. I should have known, had I not been so stupid, that this was one thing we should share regardless of anxiety or worry. Please believe me, Bruce, when I say I wanted to tell you. That's why I wrote the letter on Feb. 15th. That was the day I found out and if I could have called you that minute I would have, but after pondering over it I thought it best to let you get settled. Why? I'm afraid any reason I'd give would be inadequate according to your reasoning. I'll try to make up for not telling you by giving you a son and not a daughter!

Bruce, anything I've left unsaid (which is quite a lot), just remember I'll have it all ready to say when you're once again by my side. I love you. Simple words that mean so terribly much. Always you're in my thoughts, every minute of every day.

Yours only,

Lu

(from letter #257)

Bruce's anniversary letter was also written on their special day.

Somewhere in England, May 2, 1944, Tuesday (postmark May 3, 1944)

Dearest Lu,

All day long I have been thinking of you, and looking forward to the writing of this letter. Yesterday I decided to take a day off today, for it merited something special.

To bring you a little closer to me, I went to town and got my ring which I had left there to be engraved. The inscription looks like this: Lu to Bruce. 5-2-42.

Darling, that day was such a happy one. We drove to Troutman *(a town just on the edge of the Barium campus)* in the afternoon for something cool to drink. You wore a red skirt and a white blouse, and your hair was combed back and fell below your shoulders. You had a certain sparkle in those brown eyes, and I was so very much in love with you.

By my bed, on a little shelf by the fireplace is the miniature of you in your wedding gown. Mrs. Parcell, you are the most beautiful woman in the world. If you had not been, of course I would never have married you.

We have talked a bit about our two years. There is so much that I have left unspoken, for you might tire of my incessant love making. Lu, if I loved you then, I truly worship you now. You thought our sudden awakening surprising. It was inevitable. How I regret now that it did not happen sooner.

My love for you has increased with each passing day. You belong to me. Nothing can change that, ever. To know that and to know that you love me is a joy which cannot be surpassed. Perhaps the exception is the knowledge that you will bear our child. Lu, my happiness is dimmed only by the fact that we are separated, and that I miss you. It isn't that I am blue or too lonesome. I just miss you terribly, as I write you tonight and remember all our happy hours.

I have good faith and high hopes, darling. You deserve so much happiness and I want to fulfill that. There are so many things that I have left undone, and so many things that I want to do for you.

Lu, the fact that sometimes several days pass without my receiving any mail from you has caused me to worry a little. I'm sure you are writing and I know that it takes time for your letters to reach me, but it is only natural that I want to hear—often. Can you write every day? Even if it's only a note. Please do, if you can. Your letters mean more to me than you realize. And, darling, please tell me everything about yourself. I love you so.

All my love, always,

Bruce

(letter #258)

When Bruce received Frances's anniversary letter, he replied. He asked her if she knew what the ship builder said. This reference to a joke would come up in several letters until he finally explained it, many letters later.

Dearest Lu,

What have you done to bribe the mailman? Your letter of the second reached me this afternoon, only a week old! It was one of the best letters I have ever received from you. It was a special occasion.

You couldn't imagine how good for me it is to get letters like that. They change me completely. Today started out wrong, just like yesterday, but your letter made it a perfect day for me. You see, that is what you used to do for me, and now your letters are taking up that gap.

You feel you need me. You are deeply concerned because you may have to face this alone. Can't you see that I am with you? Every moment. We can never be "alone" again, in any way. Our life is one. That is what our marriage means to me. Our child will be the fulfillment, the consummation of that "oneness" of body, and soul, and mind. Darling, that is what makes life beautiful and worth living. That, too, is what men fight for.

And incidentally, Mrs. P, don't you remember what the shipbuilder said about the problem of the father who was unable to be present when his son was born? If you haven't heard it, have me tell you. I promise to do that. So put away the thoughts that if anything should happen, it will be your fault. You should not feel like that. I would never, never love you any less, and I must convince you of that. I mean that from the depths of my heart.

Keep your chin up, sweetheart, and please don't worry about me. I'll hurry home as soon as I can.

All my love, Mommy.

Bruce

(from letter #268)

Lots of letters were mostly chatter about everyday events. However, in this one Frances poured out her feelings.

May 10, Wednesday (postmark May 11, 1944)

Hey, you bud,

Bruce, you can't know how my heart aches for you, just as if it were a real pain. Maybe if you did know you could understand how hard it is for me to write the things I feel. Darling, you've always said I was sensitive but I'm not really. I think you're just so wonderful and good that I want to please you in every way and when I don't, it truly hurts. That's not being sensitive; it's just that I love you so much. Life without you means nothing. Sometimes it's unbearable and it takes all my will power to keep from giving up.

You prepared me so long ago for this separation and I've always been determined to make you proud of me for being a very good soldier, but I'm afraid I'm reaching the breaking point. Many a time I've been so lonely I wanted to just cry so hard until it seemed my heart would break if I didn't. Mother and Daddy are so good to me and I try not to show how unhappy I am. They are the same, and things on the surface seem the same as they did before I was married but to me nothing is right and that's because you're not here. Two women never ran a house or cooked the same way ever, and Mom and I are no exception. 'Course that's only minor, but it's an excuse for my being unhappy, when all the while it's really because I'm not with you in our apartment and doing things normally the way I've done for two years. It's strange to say but I actually feel a little like a stranger sometimes. I'm so selfish and I don't give Mom and Dad half the consideration I should, but I'm trying to do better. I've been very spiteful because I'm unhappy. I don't try to see that anyone else is happy. I need you now to scold me and make me understand I'm not the only lonely person in the world.

Living on memories is very pleasant if you can stick to memories and not think about the present. I can just see our apartment in Charlotte, even the hotel room, everywhere I've ever been with you has just been heaven. Darling, even after two years I was just as anxious for you to come home in the evening as I was after we were first married. I remember starting dinner at two o'clock in the afternoon so the time would seem short until you came home. You're such a wonderful husband. Whenever you'd comment on my cooking or my dresses or just look at me that certain way you have, of half-teasing and all serious at once, well, darling, it was just like something I'd never ever expected to come true. I can't help but remember the pest I was about your reading and sleeping. Why didn't you just beat me? I can't help but remember a few unhappy incidents either, like the time in Myrtle Beach when you got mad and I just couldn't get through to you. You crazy. Didn't you know how much I loved you? Seems to me you could tell easily enough. Sometimes I just marvel at how lucky I am. Being Mrs. Bruce Parcell makes me the proudest person ever. I'm quite conceited about you in fact. You're just the most handsome fellow I know, I mean really now!

Darling, I get lonesome just thinking about being in your arms. My heart is about to beat right out of my body. You just cause me no end of trouble. Dr. Shaw will be writing you a letter about my blood pressure.

Yours only,

Lu

P.S. I love you more than anything or anybody.

(from letter #269)

Frances was feeling lonely and worried. Here she mentioned the anticipated D-Day invasion for the first time. The newspapers were full of speculation.

May 14, Sunday (postmark May 14, 1944)

Hello darling,

Bruce, it seems that just saying I love you isn't enough. I'm that 'ole pessimist who thinks that maybe someday you'll stop believing me because Bruce, having you love me is just so wonderful yet that I'm afraid someday I'll find this to be a dream and then what would I do? You know it's a funny way to be, but sometimes I get a feeling, sort of homesickness and loneliness combined, that leaves me just without much purpose at all. Bruce, you're so much a part of me, that I can't do anything whole heartedly. I'm being a very poor sport, and especially when I know you must be having a hard time too. It isn't any good to pretend I'm cheerful all the time, because you can tell I'm not sincere. Perhaps this has just been a trying week. There has been so much talk about the invasion and although I try to ignore people's opinions and the newspapers, my attempts are pretty weak, and naturally I worry about you some. Bruce, I know you've reassured me so many times, but I cannot help it, as much as I've tried. Perhaps things will look brighter tomorrow. So I'll write again then and a longer letter. I love you dearly, Bruce. My every thought is of you.

Always,

Lu

(from letter #274)

There seems to have been no doubt in Bruce's mind that he was about to have a son. He brought up names in this letter and his old animosity towards Anne surfaced.

Somewhere in England, May 14,1944 Sunday

Hello Mom,

You have asked me a couple of times about a name for our child. I also noticed that you said, "If it is a girl, of course she will be named Ann." Well, I'm so sure that it will be a boy that I won't worry about that. Actually, if I would only admit, I'm probably a little jealous of Ann because she holds some of your affection. That's how much I love you. Don't want to share you with anyone. Please don't laugh at me for I really am that way. One of my faults that I can't overcome. So I am thinking about it, but without any success. I have an idea. Why don't you give me a list of some you have thought about, and then I'll have something to start on that I know meets with your approval.

I love you, my darling, and would give a fortune to kiss you just one time.

Always,

Bruce

(from letter #275)

On the next day, Frances wrote:

May 15 Monday (postmark May 15, 1944)

Dearest Bruce,

Surely wish you were here to enjoy the summer weather with me. It's wonderful not to have to worry with a coat. Maybe Florida weather wasn't so bad after all!

In fact I'm quite attached to Florida. You know I'm always thinking of Clearwater and the beach, but somehow my thoughts always center in Sarasota, even though we didn't stay there long. Our cute little apartment, including ants and spiders, is so vivid. I'd so love to be there now, and have you stretch out on the couch with your head on my lap and maybe tell me one of your tall tales. I never could have endured the sorrow of Fred's death if it hadn't been for you. You are so understanding, darling, about everything. I suppose I depended on you so much that now I'm just lost. Maybe the baby will teach me a little independence (until you come home 'cause I rather like being dependent on you!)

(from letter #276)

Next came a vague explanation of Bruce's trip to Italy. There was also a somewhat vague allusion to a "black Christmas present" being responsible for something. A baby on the way, perhaps?

Somewhere in England, May 16, 1944 Tuesday (postmark May 26, 1944)

Hi Mommy,

Our April showers are catching up with the schedule now, and the weather is very changeable. Nights are still cold, and of course I'm still wearing my long handles, although everyone teases me about them. You know how easily I catch cold. Well, I haven't had one since I came back from "down yonder." *(Anzio beach head in Italy)*

Suppose I tell you a little more of that episode now. Bob and I went to observe and to learn tactics, etc. I did a little flying but very little, and didn't learn much. The time away from here didn't put me behind but just a very little. Not enough to matter. It seems like a long time ago now, since getting back into the swing of things here. I knew you would be puzzled but there was nothing I could do. I tried to tell you everything I could without violating censorship.

Right now, I wish to talk about you. Remember how I used to say that "pitching woo" by long distance mail was no good. Well, you'd be surprised to know how much good it does me to just write to you. Perhaps that explains my frequent letters. However, letters don't keep me from wanting you and needing you, my darling. I'll always need you to make me completely happy, and I too, live for the day when we can be together again. And then you keep reminding me to be good, and telling me I need someone to keep an eye on me! Why, Mommy, the idea! Also, you accused me of being "a devil" for something risqué I said in a letter. Well, to tell you the truth, I do experience moments when I feel inclined to say "naughty" things to you. I restrain myself because I don't know how you might react. For example, not long ago I saw an article, with color pictures, in Colliers' Magazine about a black negligée. My reaction was to suggest to you that your black Christmas present might have been responsible for—well, you see what a devil I really am!! Lu, I can't help it. I love you so much and it's so much fun to be intimate with you. Do you mind? Tell me the truth, you bashful beauty! I love you for it though.

You be good, darling, and do take extra good care of yourself. Wish I could be there to wait on you and do things for you, just really spoil you good. I imagine your mom does a pretty good job of that!

I love you my darling, always and forever,

Bruce

(from letter #277)

Frances wrote more about the preparations she was making for September.

May 21, Monday (postmark May 23, 1944)

Dearest,

I've been quite optimistic today. Although the weather may change again I'm storing my winter clothes. As yet I haven't found where. I've never seen such a big house with so little place to put anything. Packed my wedding dress away with my future hope chest, which includes boxes and boxes of diapers, pins, blankets, sheets, pillow, material, little gowns and things. Had to sit on the chest to get it closed. Wish you could see our things. Really, I had no idea babies wore so many clothes and quaint ones, too. I'm most impatient to use them. In a way September seems awfully far away, but when I think of the things I have to do before then, it isn't long enough. It's next to impossible to buy anything for babies now and so I'll have to get busy and make some dresses. Yes, even boys wear dresses, my darling, for a little while. I promise to save his first haircut until you come home. That's your job anyway.

I'm most anxious to hear what you like for a name. Each day I decide on another. Did I hear you say you didn't like Peter? You know that was your grandfathers' name. Anne is making a baby book for us, so I had to hunt up the ancestors for the family tree. She's most determined this child is going to be a girl!

Bruce, whatever makes me love you so? You're entirely too good for me, but I'm pretty selfish and won't give you up for anything. I see you so plainly in my dreams sometimes that when I awake and find you're not really there I just have the worst feeling. Worse than any pain, because it's loneliness and sickness and a terrible longing all at once. There's no medicine for that except you here. Hurry home.

Love forever,

Lu

(from letter #284)

The baby naming issue came up again in Bruce's letters, and he was very definite in his opinions. With his being so adamant, I still wound up with the name Bruce. The Anne part was pretty much inevitable for a girl. He never did learn how to spell it.

England, May 22, 1944, Monday (Postmark May 23, 1944)

Dearest Lu,

Darling, about a name for the baby. I agree on no junior but I definitely do not want Fraley in his name. Mother would feel hurt to hear me say that, but she and all her sisters had a child with that middle name and I just don't like it. And also, no daughter with Bruce for a name, or a son either. Lu, I just couldn't, really. I never did like my name when I was young. And I don't like Ann although I know you do. But those are my true feelings and anyway I thought you were going to give me some ideas. I mean more than just one of each. I'd be satisfied with most any name you picked except Bruce, or Fraley. So you write and tell me what else you have in mind.

I wonder how you are now. And I am anxious to see some snapshots of you. I insist. How I'd love to see you, Lu! You know I love you more than anything and always will.

Be real sweet and don't fret. I'll be seeing you before you know it.

Always,

Bruce

(from letter #285)

In a long letter that Frances wrote at the same time, she briefly mentioned her worry about what Bruce was up to in Europe.

Lately they've had so much in the paper about the fighters raiding Germany and naturally I've been wondering if you were in any of them. As a rule I only scan the news because I figure (more of my logic) there's no use to ask for things to worry about. But I always have to see what kind of fighters escorted the bombers.

(from letter #286)

Bruce's letter near the end of May was meant to be reassuring. Frances had focused on Germany and had no way of knowing that he was flying missions over enemy territory in France. She was probably not pleased to learn that he had been out dancing.

England, May 26, 1944 Thursday

Hello Darling,

As for worrying about me, why I'm not worried a bit, so that should convince you. Lu, it is always hard to cope with the unknown, with something you can't understand or know about. Look at it that way and then let my reassurance comfort you. This whole business is so completely simple as far as I am concerned. I mean really!

Don't you let all you read and hear get you upset. You should know by now that our papers capitalize on the spectacular and play up all these things. I'll grant you they don't know a thing about the invasion. If there is or if there isn't one, isn't going to change my status to the great lengths that you probably imagined. No fooling, all your worrying is wasted effort.

Ahem, your old man went to a dance the night before last. We had a little squadron party. Used the ballroom of a little local hotel, and had quite a nice affair. "Doc" brought a few nurses and there were some British WAAFs present. Well, you can't really have a dance without girls and yep, I danced! My partner was a WAAF, a married one though, and we noticed right off that we wore wedding rings. She noticed my ring and asked me what kind it was. Apparently, the men over here don't wear wedding bands. Then she showed me her ring. Of course we talked about our respective spouses. And I told her about our coming blessed event. Young lady, you don't know how fortunate we were. She has been married about a year and has seen her husband only about 12 times and he is less than a hundred miles away! Anyway, we all enjoyed the dance. It was the first time I've met and talked to an English girl. They have some funny ideas about America.

Mommy, what makes you so sweet? If you were here now your sure would have trouble with me! Because I sure do love you, and miss you. But you've got to promise me you will be a better girl and stop worrying and doing so much day dreaming. Make the most of life each day. You know there is a lot of living to be done each day and it's so easy to lose sight of that. Life does have a purpose if we look on the bright side. Even if we look on the dark, serious side, it is still worth living, always, don't you think?

All my love to you, my darling and to little P, too. Goodnight,

Bruce

(from letter #288)

In this letter Frances acknowledged receiving Bruce's teasing letter about the black Christmas gift. She had news about the baby as well.

Monday May 28 (postmark May 30, 1944)

My dearest ole dope,

You're so crazy. I loved your letter today. You sounded like the old slap happy Bruce and the things you do say!! I'm blushing yet but I like you so much for being just the way you are. Perhaps I should store that black Christmas gift for future generations. There, that should hold you.

Remember the times we'd talk until the wee hours of the night? Crazy kids, but I loved every minute. When I get happy letters from you like the one today, you ole tease, I really take on new life and am more than ever determined to try and bear our separation like you want me to. And as I tried so poorly to express yesterday, the little life that has actually made itself known, and is to soon be our very own child, has made me realize that more than ever there is something to be cheerful and courageous about. It is truly the most amazing thing and I wish I could explain it to you.

 I'm being ever so good these days and your letters are tonic to me so please keep writing whenever you can. I love everything about you, poppy, and need you terribly. I'm forever yours only.

Lu

(from letter #292)

On the day Bruce wrote this next letter, he received an Air Medal, then went shopping. He tried to sound casual about it, but he must have been proud. President Roosevelt had established the medal in 1942 to be given for "meritorious achievement while participating in aerial flight." In the European theater of war, one of the criteria was flying ten combat sorties "during which exposure to enemy fire is predictable and expected." He did not share that information with Frances.

The English Coleport cup and saucer set that he mentioned is gold with aqua blue raised beads. I still have it on display in a living room bookshelf . The other notable part of this letter is that at last he told Frances "what the shipbuilder said."

Air Medal awarded to Bruce in May, 1944.

England, May 29, 1944 Monday

Dearest Lu,

We had a late supper and right after that a formation, a presentation of some awards. And your old man received the Air Medal, along with other people. Jim *(Ferguson)* was here and a couple of distinguished personages whom I can't mention here. Actually, it was nothing out of the ordinary and I am not particularly enthused about it. The Medal is quite nice, however, and I will mail it to you.

Afterwards, "Doc" Lamb and I bicycled down to a little village and did some window shopping. We found a couple of little shops with some nice things in the windows and I want to go look at them. I'm thinking of getting some china and shipping it to you in my foot locker. That would be the best way of getting it to you, I think. I haven't yet found the set I want though. I'm still finding some beautiful individual cups and saucers for your collection. I've sent three and have two more now. One is English Coleport and the other is French Cerves which Strickland says is the best china. I think you will prize them. As a matter of fact I might even brag a little and say I think they will get a place on the front row of your shelf by the mantle. You should be proud of me!

That just about covers my activities. Your letter of the 18th came just before supper and I prized it above the decoration. You sounded so cheerful and in such a good mood. That makes me happy too.

Oh, yes, about what the shipbuilder said. At least I think that's who said it. Something like, "It was only necessary to be present at the laying of the level, not at the launching of the ship." Perhaps you will have to refer back to my letter to get the significance of that. Anyway I'm terribly naughty!

Hon, I'm as happy as you are. Everything is fine. It's been almost hot today and I'm not being overworked. It comes in streaks but overall it's not tough at all. Your letters bring you right here beside me, almost, and I love you so much that I'm just happy. That's all.

You be taking good care. Don't be letting people make you exert yourself. (Here I go again.) Don't worry about mail, please. And don't let this war talk get you down. You'd probably be angry if you knew our reaction to what's being said and done at home about all this business. It's not as serious as it seems to you who are so far away. I'm being very honest, too.

I love you, you rascal. Was just thinking how shy you used to be before we were married. You're about the sweetest one

I love you and little P. too.

"P"

(from letter #293)

As Bruce was thinking about mailing china home, Frances wrote this:

May 30, 1944 Tuesday

Dearest Bruce,

Surely am enjoying your letter of yesterday. Have to read it over and over and over to keep up my morale. It's pretty good these days too, but I still have that certain feeling that I'd give anything to get rid of. It just comes in waves, and I'm afraid it will continue until I can feel your arms tight around me. Guess I'm plain homesick for you and all your foolishness. As the song goes, "I wish I could seal me up and send me off in this letter to you." All I can think of is the way you look, so handsome and so sort of rugged and the way you get so serious and then all of a sudden break into the most infectious laugh, the way you hold me so tenderly when we're dancing and oh ever so many really wonderful things about you. To boost my morale I need only to remember the private vaudeville featuring you and bath towel!

(from letter #294)

Bruce on the wing of Little Lulu, his P-47 plane.

Just a day later, Bruce wrote to describe the nose art that he had designed for his plane, a P-47 Thunderbolt. This plane was the largest and heaviest single seat, single engine fighter built during World War II. As stated earlier, it was armed with eight .50 caliber wing-mounted machine guns and two 500 pound bombs. It acquired the nickname of Thunder Monster. The pilots of the 405th flew it on low-level strafing and bombing missions in support of ground troops.

England, Wednesday, May 31, 1944 (postmark June 1, 1944)

Dearest Lu,

Perhaps, if I keep it up, I can overcome your mail shortage. Here's hoping. You will find, I believe, that mail comes in spurts. Sometimes quick, then it will take almost a month. Well, we can't have everything. I went two weeks once without a word from you, but I got over that spell.

Oh, yes, I forgot to tell you what Jim had painted on his ship. Still has I suppose. "Luger Luggin Lulu." A Luger is a German pistol. It just fitted in. I have something dreamed up for mine now. It is a picture of "little Lulu" of the Colliers cartoon, kicking a bomb off a cloud, and holding an old fashioned sling shot at the "draw." I hope you won't object. It is kind of cute. I'll send you a picture of my ship soon and you can give your approval, I hope. Out of paper, so bye now. I love you a million, trillion dollars' worth.

Bruce

(from letter #296)

Jim Ferguson, Bruce's commanding officer beside his plane that also bore Frances's nickname because "it just fitted in."

Frances was still worrying about the coming D-Day invasion and asking for help with the baby naming.

3 Wednesday, May 31 (postmark June 1, 1944)

Hello poppy,

I know I'm not half as impatient for this invasion to begin as you all are but I'll really be happy when the day arrives cause I know it will bring you nearer to homecoming. And that is what I'm really looking forward to more than anything.

Darling, what are we going to name our child! If you were here it would be so simple and we could settle it once and for all. As you have said, Sept. isn't very far off, so please let me know about this as soon as you can. After all, a name is important. I can't just start calling him "Hey you bud" or it or some such stuff. Now best you get on the ball and help me decide.

(from letter #297)

Bruce went to London for some sightseeing before the "big push" began. Travel was soon to be restricted.

England, June 2, 1944 (postmark June 5, 1944)

My Dearest,

How I miss you tonight. As I told you, Major Lamb and I are visiting London. We arrived at noon today and are staying at this hotel. *("Dorchester Hotel" is inscribed on the stationery.)* It is very nice, but it so brings back memories. We have just come in from dinner and the theatre, and I decided to write a note while waiting for him to finish his bath.

Tomorrow we will see the town—Westminster Abbey, Buckingham Palace, Waterloo and London Bridges, Parliament, and all the rest.

My every wish is that you could share this with me. I love you, Lu, and nothing can I ever enjoy as much as I could if you were sharing it. Doc and I had quite a discussion at dinner. We talked of everything under the sun, from science and medicine to religion. Why, I don't know, except that we had bottle of excellent red wine with our meal.

Sweetheart, I've learned my lesson about correspondence. Never again will I be cross in a letter to you. It takes too long to patch up our differences. Yesterday I received a letter in answer to my untimely, rather bitter note about my mail. Again I beg your forgiveness for that. Always, and forever, I love you with all my heart and soul, and nothing can change that. I so want you to be happy. How many things I have left undone and how many others I have done, which haven't been conducive to that! There has always been one thing that I have never been able to conquer, and that is my extreme jealousy. Would you love me more if I weren't that way?

Here I am rambling on about things which I wouldn't be talking about if it were not for the wine. It made me so lonesome. Also it made me want to express myself about things which I apparently cannot. My whole feeling can only be expressed by saying that to me you are life itself and that without you I am lost. My love for you is so deep that it will last for eternity.

Isn't your husband the screwiest person you know? However, unlike my bashful wife, I will read this in the morning, and then mail it.

I love you,

Bruce

(from letter #299)

Frances wrote on the day before D-Day. The "Rhyne brats" that she described were her sister Ruth's daughters, Jo Ann and Shirley.

June 5, Monday (postmark June 5, 1944)

My dearest,

Chaos has descended! We got up at six this morning to meet the Rhyne brats in Charlotte. They have grown ever so much, but are still full of the ---, and just as big a tomboys as ever. It will at least be occupation since they're here, and even thought I wouldn't admit it, I'm glad they're here.

I'm beginning to get used to not hearing so often again, but I'll never get to liking it. I'll be so happy when Sept. comes, for more than one reason of course, but mainly because my time will be so taken up that there won't be time to watch for each mail. And too, maybe this horrid, indescribable feeling I get so often, will vanish. I didn't know loneliness could be the same as sickness. Guess I'll never get used to your being away from me cause I miss you more and more each day.

Don't ever forget how much I love you and depend on you for happiness. I'm thinking of you always.

Yours only,

Lu

(from letter #300)

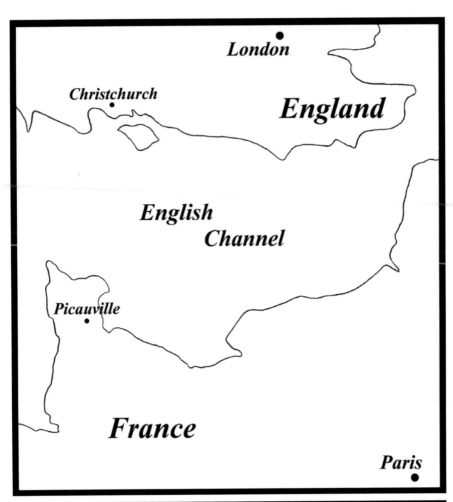

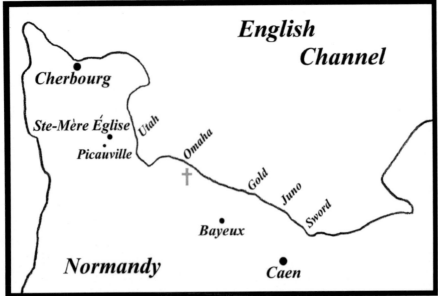

D-DAY AT LAST

Bruce's P-47 Thunderbolt, the Little Lulu. Its wings and fuselage are painted for the D-Day invasion. Planes could be identified as friendly by allied forces because of the black and white stripes.

The 405th Fighter Group continued to do fighter sweeps, escorts, strafing, and dive bombing missions over occupied France. On May 31 Bruce led fifty aircraft on an escort of B-17s to North Foreland on the southeastern coast of England. It was an uneventful mission. Tremendous troop build-up and restrictions on passes and on civilian traffic made it clear that the day of the much anticipated invasion was near. The historic allied invasion of France had begun when Bruce wrote the following letter on June 6. He, along with the rest of the 405th, was assigned to patrol duty between Christchurch and the Bay of Biscany, escorting anti-submarine aircraft. It was an important task, but the men felt left out of the main action.

England, June 6, 1944 (postmark June 6, 1944)

Dearest Lu,

Someday we will untie a blue ribbon, thumb through the package of old letters, and read this together.

This morning at nine thirty, I stood by the radio in the pilot's tent and listened to Communique Number One from London. I had just landed a short while before from a mission. We knew, officially, that the greatest operation in history was underway. My thoughts were of you, my deepest concern was your anxiety.

All along I have tried to tell you that I was safe and well, that everything was and will be ok. That is still true. Please believe me. At this moment, you have received more news, probably, than I have. You have suffered long anxious hours, but so needlessly. How I want you to believe that!

You know, your husband is almost egotistical enough to believe that this show was started for a birthday present! *(His birthday was June 10.)* Here's hoping we can see its conclusion for yours! Wouldn't that be swell?

Darling, my note last night was too brief, even for me, but yesterday was a long day for me, and I did have to get up a little early this morning. Rest assured that we are all being taken well care of, however. Please have the faith in those who are directing operations, as we do. Mr. Churchill told the House of Commons today that the Allied Armies have 11,000 first line airplanes at their disposal. That may not impress everyone, but it should have some significance for you. Everything that I have said actually amounts to "Please don't worry."

Soon I shall write more of my visit to London, but I'm sure you are not particularly interested at the moment. Nothing else has a place here, except my feeling for you. Darling, you are so dear to me. I love you with all my heart, and when we read this together, I shall love you still. You are forever in my thoughts, and that is good.

Always,

Bruce

(letter #302)

On June 6 an article appeared in a newspaper, probably the *Charlotte Observer,* dateline London. The headline announced "Airmen Express Amazement at Size of Allied Armada Hurled at Nazis." Within the article was this quote: "Major Bruce Parcell, Barium Springs, N.C., said that as the morning progressed the bad weather over France cleared to a ceiling of 3000 feet, enabling fighters to give close cover to the landing forces. Before that, he said rain squalls had blanketed the approach of the grim faced troops to the French shore." Frances was overjoyed to read this, as it let her know that Bruce was safe on that day. This was yet another story that she relished telling in her later years.

In the days following D-Day, the 405th carried out dive bombing missions in France over the Cherbourg peninsula. Fifteen pilots were killed during the month of June, a fact never mentioned in Bruce's letters home. This was Frances's reply to "the day." Had she known more about the war, she would undoubtedly been much more concerned than she already was.

June 6 Tuesday (postmark June 7, 1944)

Bruce dearest,

Guess this is the day, and even though there is a certain amount of relief to know that at last you all are getting somewhere, I can't say that I personally feel very happy about the situation. In fact I have a stronger reaction to this invasion than I did when war was declared. It just scares me to think what you all are going through. Darling, my every thought and prayer is for your safety and I have faith in you and in God, knowing you'll come through okay. It worries me naturally, when I don't hear from you but I realize that you probably weren't in a position to write and even so the mail wouldn't come through. I just wish I could help in some way so that you could come home sooner. I miss you so much. It really amazes me how much I do miss you. Nothing is fun without you.

Wed. afternoon

Well, sir, I'm just the most thrilled person you ever saw. Mom woke me up at seven this morning to tell me your name was in the paper in connection with the invasion and I nearly broke my neck getting out of bed half asleep. It was just a smidge but darling I was so relieved to have even such indirect contact with you. People have been calling me all day to make sure I saw it. I've had one ear glued to the radio all morning and still try to do my housework. I probably look like a cocked pup when the commentators mention Thunderbolts or fighter planes. Mr. Johnston was just about as thrilled to hear of you as I was. How I do hope everything works out for you and please, always remember, wherever you are, that I love you and I'm with you, not matter the distance. I'm certainly grateful to that reporter, whoever he was. It's really just too good to be true, but don't you think I'll be satisfied with just this though. I'm looking forward to a letter as soon as you can write one.

It's nearly time to go to Red Cross and I haven't begun to get ready. I will probably reach a record on dressings this afternoon cause I feel so happy and incidentally quite proud of my wonderful husband.

Darling I can't tell you enough how much I love you. Someone said it was nice for me to know you were safe and able to talk, to which I replied that you'd be talking no matter where you were or what was happening to you, but I guess someone in our family has to talk a lot! I love you and don't think for a minute I don't miss hearing all your crazy chatter and seeing your eyebrows gesticulate!

I'm yours for always,

Lu

(from letter #304)

There was more about names in the next letter, and more certainty that the baby would be a boy. Also, an article in Statesville *Daily Record* picked up on what had appeared earlier in the Charlotte paper. The writer managed to get Bruce's Air Corps career quite muddled. Frances had some fun with that.

'Barium Springs' Pops Right Out Of Invasion News From France

London, June 8. — American airmen returning from Tuesday's big invasion assault expressed amazement at the huge armada of Allied invasion craft crowding the English channel, and fighter pilots reported that no German fighter planes and scarcely any flak had been encountered.

Hundreds of Allied planes packed the air lanes. Fortresses, Liberators and medium and light bombers — many of them without escort — shuttled back and forth over the channel to drop bombs on Nazi military strongholds.

Major Bruce Parcell, Barium Springs, N. C., said that as the morning progressed the bad weather over France cleared to a ceiling of 3,000 feet, enabling fighters to give close cover to the landing forces. Before that, he said rain squalls had blanketed the approach of the grim-

faced troops to the French shore. (Major Parcell was stationed at Morris Field, Charlotte for some time and was sent from there to the Pacific when Japan attacked Pearl Harbor. He was later sent back to the states as an instructor. He has been in England for some time.

(Major Parcell is a Barium Springs boy and also a graduate of Davidson college. He was born at Cleveland and married Miss Frances Lowrance, daughter of Mr. and Mrs. J. H. Lowrance, of Barium.)

"There were enough barges so you could walk from England to France," said Pilot Capt. Jack L. Weber, Lime Rock, Conn., "and I saw only friendly planes."

Lieut. Edward Wilk, 1 Smith street, East Portchester, Conn., said: "Today it didn't seem a hell of a lot different than other days. I didn't know the invasion

had started until my ground crew chief told me when I got back. Then I felt a tingle of excitement."

"I saw more ships than I ever knew existed. Everything from landing craft to cruisers. The French shores were obscured by the smoke," said Major Garnet Palmer, Dahlone, Ga.

"I saw streams of planes in all directions," said Lieut. Walter F. Taylor, pilot, of 14 Cherry street, Milbury, Mass. "It was the damnedest sight I ever saw —unending streams of bombs rained on the targets."

Thus it went. These airmen who had been making wholesale raids on Europe for some time almost to the man expressed amazement at the number of planes and the gigantic siz of the Naval force. It gives an idea of the enormous amount of men and weapons the Allies are pouring into the western invasion.

June 8, Thursday (postmark June 9, 1944)

MY sweet husband,

I really should scold you because you didn't give me any hints as to a name for baby. After all, you're privileged to name your own child! I will send you a list of preferences though and you can do likewise. It would be too bad to pull a name out of a hat for the superior child ours will be! Darling, do help me out now because time is just flying by and September will be here before we can agree.

You're really a wonder for answering even the few questions I've asked thus far. What I would like to know though is, if you've ever received a cable from me and how long did it take to reach you? I'm looking to the future cause you know when the very special occasion arrives in September, I'll want to cable you immediately and I hope you'll let me know you know, as quickly as possible. That is of course if you aren't home by then. Wishful thinking. I really won't get my hopes up though, same as you shouldn't hope too much for a boy. My hunches have been known to be a little off. Couldn't you love a little girl just the same? As for naming the girl Anne—"of course"—well, it's just a very nice coincidence that my best friend's name is Anne (with an e) because I've always liked it very much, but, if father has strong objections then of course I'm all for naming "Anne" something else. I too feel sure we won't have to worry about that though.

Of course the *Statesville Daily* had a big write-up about Major Parcell having been quoted and as usual they got things a little mixed. In giving a sketch of your past service it seems you were stationed at Morris Field and from thence sent to the Pacific after Pearl Harbor, later being sent back to the states as an instructor and now you've been in England quite some time. You also married Miss Frances Lowrance (who is anxiously awaiting your homecoming.) Bet you didn't realize how much stir your comment about the invasion would make back home. Hope it happens again cause it certainly is a quick way to know how you are, the quickest, I suppose.

Always,

Lu

P.S. Your son is going to play half back or maybe it's fullback. I certainly have my reasons for thinking so too!!

(from letter #305)

Son or daughter, the discussion went on. Bruce did not like Anne's even suggesting what the sex of his child might be.

England, Thursday June 8, 1944 (postmark June 9, 1944)

Dearest Lu,

Received your letter of Friday, 26th today and as you say, the mail must have been held up before the "big push." Of course I have been writing, and I hope you will realize what must have happened. I'm sure mail must have been delayed for security reasons. How I hate to know that you are worrying because of it. Please don't, for I am safe and well and everything is just fine.

I think of you so much and try to picture what you are doing. I used to think that lack of patience was my one big fault, but I see that you are guilty, too. Don't think you are alone as far as this writing is concerned. Poppy is also "sweating it out." And Lu, don't worry because I have expressed my desire for a son. You know I won't be disappointed if it should be a girl. I'd like that actually, but I resent Ann's insisting on a girl! The very idea! Just tell her for me that I asked "What is she waiting for?" It's an open field, you might say.

If your mom can speed things up, well fine, but my idea is that it is such a wonderful thing to be looking forward to. Wish you would talk to me more about it. I mean intimately, about what is happening to you, and what you have to do, etc. Darling, I am so interested in your welfare and really I'm in the dark about this business of having a baby.

I love you, Lu, so very much. I think I always have, and didn't know it near soon enough. I am positive of one thing. I always will love you, to eternity. Never was I more sure of anything. Never, never doubt that. You're the sweetest one person on earth!

Always,

Bruce

(letter #306)

Mail delays made it very hard to have any kind of coherent dialogue through letters. A week and a half after D-Day Bruce had not received Frances's letter of June 6. He also announced here that he had received more medals, two Oak Leaf Clusters to add to his Air Medal. These were awarded to the holder of a medal to recognize acts entitling him to another award of that same medal.

England, June 16, 1944 (postmark June 17, 1944)

Hello Sweetheart,

I'm glad you enjoyed your trip, and you must tell me whether Dr. Shaw thought you gained too much. I sure envy you the fresh milk. That is the one thing I miss most. We've forgotten what it tastes like by now.

I'm anxious to get a letter after you learned of the invasion, to see what your reaction was. I've dreaded that time for you for I knew you would be somewhat upset about it. As I said before, it was played up too much in the papers at home. How I want you to be spared any unnecessary anxiety! That's why I keep insisting that the war is going well with us and you've nothing to worry about. And incidentally, I've gotten two Oak Leaf Clusters to the Air Medal now, but, as I said before, you can consider it all just routine. No, I'm not being modest or any such thing because it is actually "just routine."

About the time that's left for you—it is hard to realize, isn't it? And now it's only 3 ½ months instead of four. And sure, I know you miss me. I'm sure missing the greatest experience of a lifetime by not being with you through this. Still, it's good to feel that you can take it, and I know my Lu can. I've an awful lot of faith in you, darling, and you don't have to worry about my not being there. Frances told Sandy that about all he would be good for at home now would be to follow her around and push her through doors sideways! Don't you dare repeat that, but she is screwy, isn't she?

Must stop or this letter will be too heavy. Lu, I adore you and I think there is no one on earth like you. You're right about the empty feeling, but it only makes me love you more.

Always,

Bruce

(from letter #314)

Frances was getting old news as well. Here she responded to the letter about Bruce's London trip and also provided more baby news.

June 18, Sunday (postmark June 19, 1944)

Dearest pop,

Received your letter of June 2, written in London, yesterday and it has been so nice to read a little later news from you. The last letter I'd received was written May 26. I surely wish I could be with you and see the sights. Are you very far from London?

Tsk, tsk, could it have been port wine you had? You are such a crazy so and so, but I guess that's why I love you so much. I couldn't love you any more for any reason because I guess I've reached the top where you're concerned, and besides I don't want you to change any--not one bit, poppy.

Got your letter of the 5th this morning so I'm hoping to hear very soon since the invasion. It's very annoying to try to keep up with you via the news when I can't decide what Air Fore you're in. The mention of Thunderbolts keeps me jumping from 8th to 9th and I'm all confused. Can't expect much from my deductions though.

Darling, I love all the things you write. Don't stop, please. Like you, the little intimate things always make me feel so good. I only wish I could express myself as well as you do. I'm a little leery of wine. I'm afraid it would make me say things I shouldn't say in writing. Its effects are a little different on me than you!

I don't know if my letters are censored or not. Perhaps that's why I'm always a bit bashful about writing. I wish to share some things with you and you only. There are always so many things I'd like to tell you about the baby. I'm really so amused sometimes and wish so hard that you could share these things with me. At night for instance, it's amazing to be reminded so abruptly and quite vigorously, that you can't think of your own comfort entirely. It seems so silly and would look utterly foolish to anyone else, to see me lying in bed nearly laughing out loud because I've been reprimanded with a few left punches, and all because I'm comfortable on my side but "he" isn't. "He" definitely has personality already. It's such as this that seems so all important in my life now, but probably wouldn't be to you so far away. I really have a boss now but come September I'll really have my life made for me. Say, would you care for twins? No indication, pop, just a thought, and possibility!

All my love, darling.

For always,

Lu

(from letter #315)

Frances finally received Bruce's letter about dancing with the English girl. It elicited a not-unexpected reaction. The shipbuilder got a mention too.

June 20 Tuesday (postmark June 21, 1944)

My dearest,

This isn't my birthday but I feel that I'm receiving gifts, because today I've received five letters! And each one just perfectly wonderful. I feel almost as if I'd talked to you in person. I love you ever so much. I'm so happy I could just squeal! And my dear Major Parcell, you might be interested to know that you're not the only one who's jealous. Why, I'm simply seething! WAAF or no WAAF, I'm terribly glad you wear a wedding band. Not that I don't trust you, It's just that I don't want the other girls to have a chance. Don't mind me darling. I'm awfully glad you all can have dances, and you'd look awfully silly dancing with Sandy or Delashaw, but I'm truly glad "the girl" was married. Course all these facts are arguments I use on myself because I really am so terribly envious of that English girl. And don't you dare scold me about being a little mad either. I just love you so much I don't care to share you with anyone.

My mind is in a whirl. Your letters contain so much and I just absorb every word. Even your letters give me heart trouble, so just think what you in person can do!

Darn it—double darn it!! I had to walk half way home from Troutman tonight. Came to a little hill and there wasn't enough gas to get me up it and Dad isn't here to push me. He and Mom went up to the farm tonight and haven't gotten home yet. I went to Red Cross thinking I had plenty of gas. Guess I'll sit until August now since my coupons are all gone. Woe is me!

Before I have any more interruptions I want to tell you how proud I am of my husband. Congratulations, darling. You sound as if receiving a medal were nothing at all but I must tell you I think it's wonderful, and of course expected for the Major! Don't be so modest, my poppy. I feel quite egotistical myself. I've always been so proud to be your wife and you're making me prouder every day, sir. The first thing I thought of when I saw the snapshot of you on the parade grounds was, how proud I am to have such a handsome soldier for my own. Why, I'm simply beaming just thinking about you.

Darling, I promise not to worry about you. I do feel that you're quite capable and as you say, things seem worse to us here at home, because we do hear and read mostly the things that are exaggerated, and too, sometimes my imagination works overtime. I really am amazed how calmly you fellows seem to be taking the invasion. I suppose that's the very best way to do things though. At the moment I'm none too calm cause I'm terribly anxious for Dad to come home and push my car home. I feel like I've left a member of the family sitting out in the dark, all alone.

Major P., the things you do think of! I don't know about the shipbuilder, but I prefer a sponsor at the launching, but I guess I could wait until the christening if you can't make it.

I do love you, devilish as you are, and I still miss you.

Always,

Lu

(from letter #317)

Bruce continued to reassure Frances that he was doing well and not in any real danger. But he received two more Oak Leaf Clusters, which he did not earn by sitting on the sidelines of the war. Still, he called them "routine."

England, June 21, 1944 Wednesday (postmark June 22, 1944)

Dearest Lu,

Hon, we really aren't being kept too busy. Probably not as much as you would think. Of course I put in fairly long hours sometimes but it doesn't bother me in the least. Probably keeps me out of trouble!! Nope, your pop doesn't need *(to be)* kept busy for that reason. Honest!

It makes me wonder about you, the invasion, I mean. I keep trying to decide how you're reacting to it all, but I must admit that you are very reassuring and it keeps me from worrying to know you aren't worrying too much. You asked what Air Force I'm in. The Ninth, and we're pretty proud of it, too. It's newer than the Eighth, and we probably don't get as much publicity, but we get the job done just the same. I just never told you, for I've tried to steer clear of talking about my work. I've thought that the less you knew, the less you would worry about me. Oh, yes, I now have 4 oak clusters but still it's nothing but routine and well you know how I used to feel about it. You remember how I used to talk about awards.

Miss you still, sweetheart, and am hoping that Mr. Churchill's predictions of the war being over this year will come true. However, I am not going to get my hopes up yet.

I love you with all my heart, and for always,

Bruce

(from letter #318)

Frances had no idea how prescient she was being when she made mention of the baby's possibly being a girl and needing to be "modern" in her style of dress. I never did adapt to my mother's and grandmother's desires to clothe me in frilly dresses and bows.

June 23 Friday (postmark June 24, 1944)

Dearest Bruce,

Should I bring up the name business again? Darling, I wish I could know just what you like along that line. Frankly I'm not giving much thought to girls' names, nor girls clothes—comes a girl child and she'll just have to be modern from the cradle and wear pants. I'm anxiously waiting a return of the list I sent you.

I do hope you're getting mail right along cause I don't want your "morale" to suffer. I love you so much and wish always that I could be with you. You know, if I had tried, I don't believe I could have chosen a more wonderful husband. One of these first days I hope I can truly show my appreciation!

You're very, very dear to me so please take extra good care. I love you.

Mama Lu

(from letter #319)

The next day she wrote a very long letter in which she talked a lot about "baby business" and alluded to a German secret weapon that had been in the news. The Germans were developing a V-1 rocket.

June 24, Saturday (postmark June 26, 1944)

Hello my darling,

Three letters today, the last written the 16th, which has helped me no end. It was sort of a relief to hear after the invasion, although I realize war didn't start for you all on that day. I suppose I imagined things would be a little different and maybe extremely rough for you but I'm satisfied to know you're taking things only as they come.

The more I think of it the more I realize how terribly selfish I am in writing you all my problems and disturbing you, and your letters are so wonderful. Why, I'm so ashamed. Beginning now I'm turning over a new leaf and promise to be a very good girl. No worry, no loneliness, no nothing. It's more than a little hard to pretend I'm getting along splendidly without you when you and everyone else knows better. Things are looking up these days though.

Honestly, "Sonny" is having a Roman holiday tonight! Probably he would appreciate it if I'd say goodnight, and settle down. I don't know what sort of worry habits will be inherited, but, he definitely has Parcell's temperament already!

I'm thinking I have a very clever husband. The insignia, or whatever, on your plane is quite the thing. She certainly looks impish and the pilot looks the part of a movie hero! You are terribly bundled up or is that just flying paraphernalia? I do believe the English climate (or something) agrees with you. You actually look chubby.

Regardless of how routine it is to win an Air Medal, I'm very proud of you and think you're pretty special. So does Junior! We've decided father will just have to get on the ball and come home immediately following the launching cause even though you won't be of any actual help at the time, I hate to miss hearing how you paced the floor etc. as an expectant papa. And besides, there's so much fun to this that we don't want you to miss it!

My sweetheart, if you didn't write such ardent letters and tell me exactly how you feel, I'd be most unhappy. I regret that it isn't in my making to express myself as freely. I idolize you so that it seems utterly fantastic still that you could have wanted me for your wife. I promise you this though. Upon your return you'll find the most devoted little family ever.

As for being in the dark about this baby business, you know it's quite new to me too! And I don't say I understand half that is happening to me, but it has become so normal that anymore I don't give a thought to the foods I should eat, the pills I take, the kind of exercise I'm supposed to do. The only thing I really am conscious of is trying to train my "mentalities" to work on an unusually cheerful basis and at times that's terribly difficult.

I'm learning to take the news with a grain of salt. If I didn't, I'd forever be in frenzy! It's better if I just keep up with the headlines and let you supply me with bits of news. I haven't given special attention to the German "secret weapon" because it's a little beyond me, and it seems that thus far, it hasn't been too successful.

I really must stop this letter. It's getting to be a book. Don't forget how much I love you, darling. I'll keep my chin up so long as I have your wonderful letters and snapshots to ponder over and I'll be good, sir. We'll be so happy again, and I hope it won't be too far off.

Yours always,

Lu

(from letter #320)

Bruce's first mention of France was in this letter, along with some confusion about the newspaper article that quoted him after D-Day.

England, June 25, 1944 Sun. (postmark June 26, 1944)

Dearest Lu,

Lu, I landed in France yesterday and was on the ground a few hours. It was a very interesting experience and added to the tall tales I am saving to tell you. Don't worry, it was routine and worked out very smoothly. I ate fresh eggs, over light, with crisp bacon, jam, crackers, and hot coffee with sugar and cream! How about that? The trip was uneventful, both ways. That is about all I can say here.

You still have my curiosity aroused about the statement I made on D-day. I didn't make any statement! So I'm anxious to see what that guy dreamed up. How about sending me the clipping?

I still want to know why you can't write the things you would tell me if I were there. No one but me reads your letters.

Be sweet, darling, and keep happy.

All my love,

Bruce

(from letter #321)

He wrote a rare letter to his sister Blanche on the same day as he wrote the previous letter. The trip to France must have been more important than he let on.

England, June 26, 1944, Monday

Dear Blanche,

Your letter of the 12th arrived today, and I'm sure you will be surprised to find me answering it so soon. I've neglected everyone but Lu and I am proud of having written to her as often as I have.

Yes, the big show is finally under way. I am glad to be a part of it, but am looking forward to the day when it is over. It is on a scale never before seen, and is inconceivable even to us who are close to it.

I landed in France on Saturday and was there for a few hours. That is about all I can say except that I was close to the War. Everything is going along very smoothly for me. No, Jim isn't here. He was transferred some time ago but he comes in occasionally to fly with us. Incidentally, I have the Air Medal with four Oak Leaf clusters now, but as I tell Lu, it's strictly routine and nothing at all out of the ordinary. I have a lot of tales to tell someday, but can't relate them here.

I'm well, Blanche, and living very comfortably. Lu seems to be well and happy and the little one apparently is coming along satisfactorily. That is a great consolation to me, naturally. We're having trouble with names now. Any suggestions? Write again.

Love,

Bruce

(from letter #322)

Food was good, apparently. And at last Bruce discussed baby names that he preferred. Not that it was going to make any difference.

England, June 26, 1944 Monday (postmark June 27, 1944)

Dearest Lu,

Today has been dark and dull, with rain. I was up very early—4 o'clock—but back to bed at six, and slept ever so long. After lunch, Ralph Jenkins, "Doc" Lamb, and several others rode into town for a movie—"Buffalo Bill." You know, a good old "shoot 'em up," cowboy and Indian affair, in color. Were home in time for super—roast beef, mashed potatoes, cabbage, corn and lima beans, bread and butter, coffee and pears for dessert. Do you wonder sometimes what we're doing? Well, it's this way. When we aren't working, we try to make the most of everything and get away for a little relaxation. Of course, my activity is confined to just such recreational pastimes and my social life passed out of existence one Sat. noon when you drove away in a little green Buick. That seems such a long time ago, too. No, my sweet, I'm not complaining one bit about my living. It could be much, much worse, I know.

Incidentally, the little one must be getting to be quite a fellow from the way you talk. If I were there I sure would tease you, you rascal. I'm so glad you are happy about the whole thing. I don't ever want you to be any other way.

No, I didn't mean to save that certain garment *(the black Christmas negligée)* for future generations. I meant save it for us. And no, you can't make me blush. Just try and see!

My love to the folks, Lu. Tell them to keep on taking extra special care of you for me. I love you, darling, and I too, need you and always will.

Always,

Bruce

(from letter #323)

This next commentary was written on the back page of the June 16 letter.

From your list of girls' names, I like Jeanne, Susan. One of my own would be Joan but not Jane, please. How about Lu? That's awful cute, don't you think? Or Frances, at least for a middle name.

For the boy, of course, it's hard for me to decide. Certainly not the usual names like Robert, John, Charles, and Bill, etc. Especially Charles. That wouldn't do any more than Cornelia would for a girl! *(Possibly Cornelia was the aforementioned "San Antonio rose" whom he met in Texas. There is a picture of a woman named Cornelia in a scrapbook kept during Bruce's Randolph Field tenure.)*

I like Michael, Peter. How about Don? I think a short name, one that is masculine is the best. Like you, I feel that we haven't found it yet, but I will not worry. Suppose you go ahead and make your decision and let me know. I'll tell you if I don't like it. That seems the best way. Then it will be all settled.

I love you, Mommy.

Mr. P.

(from letter #323)

Frances's letter of June 29 *(letter #326)* was not especially noteworthy, but Bruce had written himself notes on the back of the envelope:

1 Talk to Davenport and Logan-Get the Sqdn. some publicity.

2. Group reports are too conservative on our results. Let's have credit for what we do.

3. Gonzales, take some pictures of 510th sqdn. at once.

The baby naming issue would not go away.

June 30, Fri. (postmark June 30, 1944)

Dearest Major P,

Blanche just called, wanted to know if I'm interested in going to the beach. Surely am but I'm afraid that's as far as we'll get. She said they had a letter from you today, with pictures of "little Lulu." Guess I'll go over there on Tuesday if nothing happens. I get such a kick out of Blanche. She is almost as screwy as another Parcell I know. Hope I can remember her wild tales to tell you. Today she said she felt as if she should have a medal just for being your sister!

There's still lots of packing away to be done in order to make room for "Junior's" things. For the life of me I can't figure out where we picked up so much stuff and just think what we 'll have to move next time. Gosh, ain't it awful!

I've been studying the name book again and per usual am quite confused. It gives the meaning and derivation of each name and there are some names—Cadwallader, Eustace, Isadore, Halbert, Llewellyn, Sebastian, Orville (that's my favorite. I'm christening our little lamb, the one Mom gave us for Christmas) and so on. Perhaps Blanche can help us decide on a name. I'm sure it would be original if she picked it. Bruce means positive, daring and is of Gaelic origin. According to my names I'm free and dignified!

There's work to be done, father, so until tomorrow, stay out of mischief (don't forget my jealous nature either!). I love you. Wish I could tell you how very much.

Yours always

Mrs. P.

(from letter #327)

Here is Frances's first letter to be returned and marked as "Missing!" That meant that it was also the first one that Frances wrote which Bruce never received. From now on, she was writing to him, but he did not receive any more of her letters. By the time they reached France, he had been killed in action. She continued to get letters up through July 23, probably the last day he wrote. After that, there was only silence. The "Missing in Action" telegram did not arrive until August 11.

July 1, Sat. (postmark July 1, 1944)

Hello, Major P.

How I can possibly miss you more each day is something I'll never be able to solve. But it is a fact, and you may as well know it, my dear ole fud, because I can't pretend to be free from worry and act as if I'm sitting on top of the world, when all the while my every thought is of you. Best you give me another scolding, poppy. I'm in a very rare mood today.

Mom and I played hooky from the children last night and saw a very entertaining movie and I've made some "discoveries" or maybe I'm shaping Junior's future personality. At any rate Harry James certainly has a restful effect on "his" movements, but Spanish music definitely he dislikes. The classical type music is also a favorite for slumber and gives Mrs. P. no end of comfort. This sounds terribly screwy, but so help me it's the truth. Do you think I should try reading Shakespeare or Shelley or maybe Mary Roberts Rinehart, just to get a few impressionistic reactions? I need not fear how intelligent he will be because according to my calculations he's bound to inherit father's mind and handsome features. Maybe Mom will just contribute to his practical nature. I'm terribly curious as to the outcome, aren't you?

Had a very good dream last night but alas, I doubt if it comes true. You arrived home only two months after the baby was born and everything was just perfect! See can you do, pop! One little ray of happiness that touched me today was the fact that my accounts checked to a tee. I don't mean to boast but it's ever so seldom that they do. Proves how efficient I can be when there's no "disturbing" influence! I'd really rather have you here though than to have my checkbook come out even. See how much I love you?

I love you, a whole dollar's worth. And I feel much, much happier just having written you.

I'll always love you.

Mamma P.

(from letter #328)

By June 28 Bruce had just received Frances's letter from June 19. Mail delivery continued to be a problem.

England, June 28, 1944 (postmark July 2, 1944)

Dearest Lu,

How are you, honey? I didn't write last night, and even now, my letter will be quite dull. That's the way the weather is, and how we feel—a little on the dull side. I have another fire tonight to take the chill out of the room, and in June! Why don't you ship me a few little sunbeams.

Hon, I sure will be glad, too, when you tell me that you have received some letters written since June 6th. You know, you remarked that you didn't know whether your letters to me were censored or not. I've told you that they were not, in at least two letters. If someone hasn't been sending my letters through to you, I'm going to be very unhappy. Anyway, you go ahead and say just what you like, and don't worry about it. It's so good to have you tell me about the baby. It keeps me from wondering sometimes whether it's true or not, about us, I mean having a child.

Lu, please forgive this letter. It must be very stupid, but I've too much competition with a couple of crazy men in the room telling jokes, etc. and teasing me about having twin girls.

I love you, Lu, so very, very much. Please stay well and take good care of yourself.

Always,

Bruce

P.S. Please send me four sheets. It's impossible to buy any over here. I prefer the narrow ones. BFP

(from letter #329)

July 2, Sunday (postmark July 3, 1944)

Dearest Bruce,

They just said over the radio, "Have you written to that service man today?" I did write but was interrupted so much that I'm starting afresh. Wrote you a note at midnight last night, but mostly for my own peace of mind. We were having a terrible electrical storm and I felt in the need of company and the kind of comfort you used to give me during thunderstorms. At any rate I went right off to sleep afterward, so maybe it was sort of a new type of mental telepathy. I kinda believe in that stuff! I say a prayer each night that you'll come home soon, and then I just put myself to sleep saying, "Bruce, please come home soon." Not that I don't have any faith in my prayers. The wishing is just for good measure.

Shirley keeps pestering me to play and sing some, so it looks as if I'll have to or else not get any peace! The piano really is a joy to play, and Sundays seem to be the only time I can find to play anymore. Don't ask me what I do. This big house is something else to keep straight. I'll really appreciate the compactness of a little place again.

Bruce, I love you. Seems as if I always have. There's never been anyone but Bruce, it seems. And I always will love you with all my heart. Guess you know I'm always thinking of you.

Always,

Lu

(from letter #332)

England, July 5, 1944 (postmark July 6, 1944)

Hey Mom,

This will let you know I'm still thinking of you, and that everything is fine. It's sack time again for me in a very few minutes, so I'll be short and sweet. Especially sweet, I hope.

Hon, incoming mail is very uncertain and I'm not getting your mail, but I know it's on the way and pretty soon now it will be coming in again ok. I have a lot to look forward to, so I'm happy. Just don't want you to worry or think I'm not answering your letters.

You must think I'm pretty bad for not helping you any more than I have on a name for the young one. Hope you got my letter on that subject. And it's not that I'm not interested. You know that. But in the final analysis, it's going to be your decision. If Lu decided on Ebenezer I think I'd like it. That's because I love you, darling, and that's for sure! As a matter of fact, I still say you're the sweetest person in the world and always will be. You may not know it but you strictly have me in the palm of your hand. And I even dreamed about you last night (You should be blushing!!) You mean more to me now than anything possibly could, and my every wish is to hold you close to me again.

You see what I mean by "sweet." Be good, darling, and have patience. We have a lot of things to look forward to.

All my love,

Bruce

Lu, be careful about addressing my letters. Several have been mis-sent because they read the number wrong. You make a four that looks like a seven, and these postmen aren't too careful. Mr. P.

(letter #334)

July 5 Wednesday (postmark July 6, 1944)

Dearest Bruce,

This will only be a beginning 'cause it's late again and I must get in my rest! I have been to Cleveland today and just got in. Had a grand time there. Blanche is a scream. Will tell you more about it tomorrow. I'm feeling a little lonely. There's such a gorgeous moon, and no good husband to pitch woo with! I love you until I think it's really wrong to care so much for one person, but it's just something about you, sir, that I can't resist.

Blanche fixed us all a mint julep (mine was really mostly water) this afternoon and I think it must just now be taking effect because I feel highly sentimental and yet, somehow I believe I always feel that way but am a wee bit bashful about setting it down on paper. If I could just slide down in bed and be sure your arms would be around me I would be more anxious to retire. As it is, I'm quite weary but still not sleepy enough to fall asleep without being a little thoughtful about the happiness I once felt when you were here beside me. Oh, Bruce, don't scold me for being blue. I do miss you in ever so many ways and although I'm getting along fine and my spirits are good, at the same time I lack the spark and interest in life that you always supplied for me. I like every little thing about you and hate to miss being with you during the present crisis because I know you must be changing in little ways, perhaps not noticeable to you. In other words, I hate being away from you even when you change an opinion. I love you that much.

Do hope the mailman favors me today. Hope you're still having time to enjoy life too. I love you darling. My highest ambition is to see you home again soon.

Always yours, Lu

(from letter #336)

The name question persisted. No girl names were being considered here.

Envelope labeled "Missing!"

July 8 Saturday (postmark July 8)

Dearest,

You know, I've been thinking quite seriously about the name again and your family has been no end of help. As usual I'll give the suggestions and you tell me what you think. Did you consider Paul? I'm a little partial to Michael Lee, Peter (or Paul) Scott (Blanche's suggestion) and I do like Don, but I'd like another name too. In fact the name we finally decide is the best will probably sound as if it were the one all along. Just have to make up our minds which is which. I'm beginning to narrow it down to just a few now.

(from letter #336)

Frances kept crackers by her bed for eating first thing in the morning. She must have been suffering from morning sickness, even seven months into her pregnancy. She was not happy with her appearance either.

Envelope labeled "Missing!"

July 10 Sunday (postmark July 10, 1944)

Dearest Bruce,

Oh, dear. I'm so uneasy. A little mouse just ran in my room and I can't find him anywhere. Now I'll be awake half the night wondering where he is and what he's doing. Although I have five pictures of you in the room, it doesn't seem to have the desired effect on mice. He's probably after my crackers I keep by the bed for my "before rising snack."

Darling, I have been trying to collect a few razor blades before mailing a box but things over here are just scarcer than hen's teeth to find, and when you do find them you have to practically kill the clerk before she will sell you anything. Perhaps I'll get a few things together this week.

Bruce, if I can possibly find some film (that too is just extinct) I will send you some snapshots, although I'd really rather save them for the baby pictures. No, I'm not ashamed for you to see me. I'm just glad you don't have to, 'cause I do look quite "shapeless" and haven't yet gotten used to this bulkiness. I don't mind of course, but then you can see how I would feel about it. Clothes nowadays are somewhat concealing but you must remember that a person this close to the "end" can't very well conceal, and I do try so hard to look presentable. Right now I envy those slender gals but pretty soon they'll be envying me! Consolation enough, I think. You are mighty right, we'll have to do this again but not too soon and not just for your benefit, sir!! The idea! Darling, I do wish you were here now. I love you so much, and it is so hard not being able to share this first experience with you. Time can't pass too fast until you come home again.

As for the date of arrival, Sept. 27th is supposed to be correct but one never knows about these things. I'm hoping for a little earlier arrival instead of a late one. Naturally I'm terribly curious already.

I love you dearly. Just thinking of you gives me such an odd feeling. Do hurry home.

I'm yours always,

Lu

(from letter #337)

Jim Johnston, son of orphanage superintendent J.B. Johnston and brother of Frances's good friend Leila, lay seriously wounded somewhere in Europe. Frances hoped that Bruce could find out some information about his condition.

Envelope labeled "Missing"

July 11 Tuesday (postmark July 11, 1944)

Dearest Major Bruce,

You all really must be taking a rest. I haven't seen any accounts of flying for a long time. Don't get out of practice now. I'm ever so curious about all your missions, but naturally I don't expect to get an account until you come home. Blanche said she'd surely like to know what you've "shot down."

Mr. Gardner came by this morning to check up on the piano and give it a tuning but I postponed that until fall when it will need it again anyway. They're awfully nice about looking after it. I guess I've enjoyed playing it more than I have enjoyed anything since you left. It really has a lush tone and is ever so handsome. Mom says this is the time when I should shape my child's abilities! Course I don't believe any of that stuff, but I guess it does help my disposition, which in turn has favorable effects of the little one. They tell me the father has something to do with what the child is and does, so I needn't worry too much about his personality!

It would be ever so nice to be able to write down the baby's name and not have to call "it" he or her! I'm pretty partial to Michael Lee myself and even "Mike" is kind of a cute nickname. If the baby were born tomorrow we'd have to decide in a hurry so let's just pretend a little while that he is arriving quite soon, so maybe we can make up our minds in a hurry and definitely. You know the announcements have to be made out a little in advance anyway--the kind I want. Shows how positive I am about its being a boy!

I'm sending you Jim's hospital address so that if by any slight chance you can contact him, you will know where to locate him. Surely hope they hear soon where he's wounded. Mrs. J.B. is so worried.

Darling, you take extra good care of yourself. I love you so much. Nothing will ever be the same until you come back.

Yours always,

Lu

(from letter #338)

THE WAR IN FRANCE

On July 5 Bruce was still in England. By the time he wrote again on July 10 he was in France. The entire Fighter Group had moved from Christchurch to Normandy. The Army constructed an airstrip in just one day near the tiny village of Picauville. It was made of a prefabricated bituminous surfacing commonly called Hessian matting. The pilots referred to it as tar paper. Named A-8, the airstrip was bulldozed out of a former apple orchard. Many villagers came to watch this spectacle. At that time most of the farmers in the area were still plowing their fields with horses. They had never seen a tractor, let alone a bulldozer.

The airstrip was perilously close to the front battle lines, so pilots had to take off towards Utah Beach to avoid anti-aircraft fire. They then flew back across the German front lines towards St. Lo and Coutances to attack rail lines, boxcars, tanks, trucks, and troop areas. Pilot Ralph Jenkins recalled, years later, "At our base near St. Mere Eglise, we were so close to the front lines that we could hear the rumble of artillery duels. We had to circle over the field to gain the 10,000 feet needed to cross the front. We'd be bombing and strafing within ten minutes."

Another pilot, Charles Mohrle, told the story of local families coming out to watch the planes taking off. They would stand very near the end of the runway, which was extremely dangerous. The pilots found a local priest who spoke some English and told him to explain the danger so that people would move further away. The priest translated, then came back to say, "They said to tell you that they trust you." These people had been living under German occupation for four long years and saw the Americans as their saviors.

Somewhere in France, July 10, 1944 (postmark July 12)

Dearest Lu,

How time does fly! Your mail has been slow and I haven't been writing very often, so we can look forward to our mail when things start running smoothly again. Don't think I've written for 3 or 4 days now.

Everything is still going along fine, as you probably have seen in the papers. Wish I could tell you about the things I am doing and seeing, but that can all wait.

Right now I'm interested in some late news from you. Received your letter of June 21st with the snapshot of you. You look fine, "Mama P." and that is good. You must be having fun basking in the sun. I've been almost cold this evening with a heavy jacket on. We've had some "exceptionally" cool weather lately.

Lu, it's getting almost too dark to see how to write. I have a lovely view from where I'm sitting. Remember to ask me sometime where it was.

I love you, Mrs. P. and am getting to miss you more and more. Not that I haven't always, but—you know how it is. There will come a day, though and we will have years and years to make up for all this.

Keep smiling, darling, and keep our morale up. Take care of yourself and Little P. and be sweet. How is little P, Mommy?

All my love, always,

"Pop"

(from letter #341)

Envelope labeled "Deceased!" That is crossed out and it is stamped "MISSING"

July 12, Wednesday (postmark July 13, 1944)

Dearest pop,

A letter today! It does me ever so much good to receive a little word from you. Can't imagine why you aren't getting my letters now. I haven't missed but a very few days, writing to you. Maybe you'll get a lot at one time.

Dad and I went to prayer meeting tonight. First time I've been in weeks. We decided a watermelon would taste good this hot evening, so Dad took it upon himself to go get one. It really was delicious. I missed you, so I ate some for you! There's surely nothing wrong with my appetite.

The Parcell clan is coming over tomorrow so Mom and I have been making some preparations tonight so we can really sew tomorrow. I really think your mother is getting a little worried about the future grandson's wardrobe. Naturally nothing worries me, but I am sewing quite furiously all the time.

Mom started fixing the bassinette today and it's going to be ever so pretty—gets me all excited to hurry and get it "filled." This is ever so much more fun than planning one's trousseau and that is quite an experience. I'll never forget how modest I was in selecting things for my trousseau. Some beautiful things I would love to have had, but couldn't quite bring myself to choose those less conservative models! Guess I've changed a little. You should see my new trousseau! (Hope you're blushing).

I love you as you are and I'll always love you. As you know, there's a very special place in my heart for you, so hurry home sweetheart and help ease the loneliness that's become a habit with me.

Yours only,

Lu

(from letter #342)

Envelope labeled "Missing"

July 13 Thursday (postmark July 14, 1944)

Dearest poppy,

I'm sitting here looking at the handsomest man there ever was and he has the nicest little boy grin I ever did see. Just from looking at him gives you a faint idea of how really nice he can be and what a lot of fun he is. There's ever so much devil in his eye and I imagine in his manner, because just the cock of his head gives that impression. But you can also tell he's very precise and emphatic, just by the way he ties his tie just so, and pins his insignia on in the exact spot. No doubt he's very kind to little children and very considerate of old ladies and is probably the young girls' dream, but somehow I really don't care for him so much, because, you see, he can't talk, nor walk, nor dance and he certainly can't pitch woo. And it's a fact he wouldn't be good pinching material and teasing wouldn't even faze him, but if he were real instead of just a picture, OOO-OO-OO-What a man! I have a husband that fills this description, only better, but he's ever so far away and I miss him something fierce. In fact I feel like weeping just for the simple reason that I love him so much and can't seem to do a thing about it except tell people what a wonderful fellow he is, and all about the things he likes and dislikes and why. There's no end of pleasure in talking about your husband especially to someone who can retaliate with a little story of his youth! Darling I haven't been drinking, nor do I have the slightest idea why I'm carrying on this way (perhaps I'm boosting my morale via the "think as such and ye shall be" theory. In other words if I sound crazy enough I might work myself out of an oncoming case of the blues!)

Your mom and Blanche were here today and telling all sorts of incidents about you when you were just a tot and how you didn't have any hair until you well over a year old! That's quite serious, Major P. Do you think the little one will stay bald headed that long? Guess he'll have to have a toupee.

Frankie and Bill *(her brother Skinny's wife and baby)* got home last night but we haven't seen them yet. They're staying only two weeks and plan to come up here the first of next week. Can't wait to see Bill. Frankie is a little worried for fear Skinny is going overseas, so she doesn't want to stay too long. Can't say as I blame her but I do hope, for Mom's sake mostly, that he won't have to go. Guess the worry would just about kill her. You'd think she'd raised you from the cradle, the way she worries, but of course I'm always pointing out how needless it is. She's just a natural born worrier and it can't be helped.

There's the grandest drizzly rain on the tin roof, so nice for sleeping, and I'm not a bit sleepy. If you were here, I'm afraid I'd pester you so that you couldn't sleep either. My nature, pop. Junior also thinks this is a grand night for sleep, already so much like you it's remarkable! I'd love a good night kiss, Major P. but I'll wait until you return for that.

I love you,

Mrs. P.

(from letter #343)

On July 16 Bruce received a promotion to Lieutenant Colonel, effective back to July 6.

Somewhere in France, July 16, 1944 (postmark July 18, 1944)

Dearest Lu,

This has been quite a day. A most unusual day, as you will see in a moment. It is Sunday and although the weather was bad this AM, the sun broke through this afternoon, and it is actually warm again.

First of all, I got a bath this morning. Now that may not sound so unusual to you but to us here it is a luxury. Later on we will be a little better set up for that, but right now we are "roughing it." However, the food is good or at least the fresh air around here gives me an awful appetite. I'm getting to be a confirmed "chow hound."

To make it a really perfect day, I received two letters today from you, June 27th and 30th respectively. One contained the snapshots taken at Ann's. For some reason, letters over here mean so much more than they ever did before in England. When I hear from you, it is so much easier for me to answer. Perhaps they bring you a little bit closer. I know they do, especially with the pictures.

And, just incidentally, your pop was promoted today. Bob called me over and, as is the custom, gave me a "talking to" and then gave me the order. So consider yourself Mrs. Lt. Col. B. Parcell! Actually, I feel a little bit unworthy, or something of the sort, but am actually pretty excited about the whole thing. And I didn't even have any silver leaves to put on! But I'll get some, and quick. The promotion was effective July 6th, but was a little late in catching up with us.

Lu, my letter may be short, but that doesn't mean I love you any less. I'll get back to some good long "mushy" ones real soon when things settle down a little.

I'm still fine and dandy and I have written to Mother. Will try to keep it up.

I love you, darling, and still say you're the sweetest one person in existence. Honest. I really mean it.

All my love,

Col. P.

(letter #345)

By July 20 Frances knew that Bruce had moved to France. She talked here about Jim Johnston again. His brother Joe was also in the military as was his sister Leila, who was in the WAVES, the women's branch of the Navy Reserves.

Envelope labeled "Missing!"

July 20, Thursday (postmark July 20, 1944)

Dearest Bruce,

More confusion! Naturally my curiosity is very keen anyway, about all the things you're doing, but when your "position" suddenly jumps from England to France and I've missed receiving the letters in between, well, I'm befuddled! I'm being presumptuous in believing it isn't a permanent change since your address is the same but then, I don't know.

I hated to get up this morning because I just knew there wouldn't be a letter for me, but I was pleasantly surprised. It's ever so good to hear again. You've told me I shouldn't worry when I don't hear from you, but I can't help it a little bit. You probably know what a lonesome feeling you get when there's no mail.

The Johnstons still haven't heard any more about Jim. Joe's wife has been sent back to the states, and she and Leila are coming home tomorrow. I'm anxious to see Leila in her uniform. I'm glad they're coming now. It will help Mrs. Johnston so much. This uncertainty is really terrible for them.

Your son is starting early fall football practice today! I've never seen such vigor! No wonder I'm ready to collapse at the end of the day. I've been hoping the doctor and I have made a mistake about the date and that "he'll" arrive a month early. I'm just so impatient! According to my way of thinking he will help me pass the time more quickly until you come home. I'm passing it now but that would be ever so much more pleasant.

As usual I've been changing my mind about the name again. I've called the "unknown" by Michael for long enough to wonder about it. I'm thinking maybe Peter sounds less "sissy" and just from observation, this fellow isn't going to be a sissy by any means!

By the way, in a spare moment I wish you would write out a list of the people you want to send announcements to, but think of everybody, because I remember about "all those people" you forgot when we were mailing wedding announcements.

I feel more than a little detached from you, poppy. Guess that comes from not hearing from you, but the letter today has helped. Wish I could tell you how much I love you. Remind me someday to do that, will you?

Be a good boy, pop.

I love you,

Lu

(from letter #348)

Tidbits about Bruce's role in D-Day surfaced here.

France, July 20, 1944 (postmark July 21, 1944)

Dearest Lu,

Time certainly has flown these past few weeks. That is always the case when something new and different is happening, and you are busy, too. I have not been writing as often as I'd like, and it worries me a little, for I know you will worry, too, if my letters don't come.

Perhaps the enclosed money order will help to "soothe" your anger, if any, with me. I have no need for money, having spent not one cent since I've been in France. I'm also returning the clippings, as you asked me to. They sure did get things confused, don't you think? Incidentally, I didn't say that about the weather, and someday I'll explain why. I was flying on D-day, but probably not as you might have suspected. I got a bigger thrill the day before on a mission in France. We had an important target and hit it, too. Also, I never saw as many boats in all my life, as I saw that evening in the Channel, on my way home.

I've had an opportunity to see a little of the French countryside. It is somewhat similar to England, but the French people on the whole seem entirely different. I think I would like France if it were not for the effects of German occupation, and the war. In a way, France is to be pitied. She has suffered much, and will, until this is over. The people I've seen appear friendly enough, but I trust no one at this stage of the game.

We have a nice place here, and living conditions are going to be ok. Our food is good and we live comfortably. The weather continues to be bad--lots of rain and cloudy weather. That has direct results on the course of the war, too. That is enough about that.

A little while ago I was over in the pilots' tent listening to Fred Waring on the radio. We get excellent music—"Command Performance" and other special programs for the Armed Forces. It makes me think back, though, to better days. Also, I look forward to the same.

How is Mom? Mail is still a little slow, but that will work out in time. I sure enjoy your letters to the utmost and I miss you darling, more and more.

Hope you haven't suffered too much from the heat. The paper says it's been awfully hot this summer.

Mom, if I keep on, this letter will be too fat for the clippings and money orders. Sure would like to see you and I'm beginning to realize that Sept. is really just around the corner. I'm prepared though! I want you to know how much I love you, and need you, darling. Please write just as often as you can and don't worry about me for I'm ok. Incidentally, I completed 6 years' service on the 10th, and will draw an additional 5% of my pay. Little P. is practically educated already!

All my love,

"Col. P."

(letter #349)

This is the last letter Frances received from Bruce. She would write eleven letters to him after his death. The "Missing in Action" notification did not come until August 11, 1944.

France, July 22, 1944 (postmark July 23, 1944)

Dearest Lu,

Another dull, damp day, but I've managed to keep dry. You must be reading about the bad weather.

We were quite cheered up with fresh apple and raisin pie for supper. Food here really has been good. We've had hot biscuits, even!

After supper tonight I had my hair cut by one of the enlisted men in the squadron. He did a very good job, too. Would have had a hot shower, but it was a little too cool outside. Right now I'm sitting on an ammunition box (empty, of course) and using an improvised table.

You asked about Sandy. He left for England yesterday, for a few days leave. He is ok though. I hope to take a few days off soon. Not that I'm overworked, but it is good to get away once in a while.

How is everything? I'm really beginning to miss your letters now, but am expecting the mail to start pouring in soon. Would like some late news of developments and how you are. I'm not going to worry but I sure am "sweating it out." Sept. sure is close now.

Hon, I'm short of paper (poor excuse.) I love you more than ever, sweetheart, and sure do miss you. Yes, I can read between the lines. I feel the same way, only more so.

Always,

Bruce

(letter #351)

This letter brought the news of Jim Johnston's death. Of course, Bruce never knew of it, as he did not receive the letter.

Envelope marked "Deceased!" This is crossed out and it is stamped "MISS-ING"

July 24, Monday (postmark July 24, 1944)

Dearest Bruce,

Have been waiting to write until after the noon mail, thinking I might get a letter, but no such luck. Someone said the mail had been held up again so perhaps that's it. Hope you're receiving my letters by now though.

You know I wrote you that Jim was wounded on the 20th of June. Well, the Johnstons received a message this morning that he died nine days later. Mother and Ruth have been over there nearly all day. I do wish there was something I could do, but Mom thinks it best if I stay here and I guess she's right. It's a shame Leila couldn't have stayed over but she's coming back in several weeks, so maybe that's better. There is a terrible feeling of doom around the house. I must write to Leila this afternoon. I think the family is more worried about Dee, Jim's fiancé, than they are anyone else.

Mom and Dad are going down to see Frankie and Bill tonight before they return to Texas. Skinny writes that he surely does miss them. I can see where little Bill would leave a gap in his life! He's so cute.

Darling I feel rather far away from you, not knowing any recent news of you. Take special care of yourself, for us. We love you more than just words can express. Only seven more weeks and little P and I will both be writing you. I love you, Bruce.

Lu

(from letter #353)

A letter from "Mother Lowrance" never arrived because it was returned as undeliverable, as so many of Frances's letters had been.

Envelope marked "Deceased!" This is crossed out and it is stamped "MISSING"

Sun. July 23rd 44 (postmark July 25, 1944)

Dearest Bruce,

We wish so much you could be here this bright Sunday afternoon. We think about you all thru the days. We appreciated your writing to us before you went over and thought every day I would write. Frances is just fine. She has a good appetite and looks well. She is sewing some and helps me lots. It means a lot to us to have her here. If you could be here too we would all be so happy. Frankie and Bill spent a few days with us last week. Bill is such a sweet baby and good looking too. They are going back on the plane about next Wednesday. Don't worry about Frances. We are taking good care of her and she is under a good Dr. She looks forward to your letters and they mean a lot to her .Do hope it will not be so long till you will be at home.

Son, I did appreciate the pitcher you sent me. It is lovely, the very prettiest one I have. I guess Frances told you I got a new "what not." And that is where I put my pitchers.

Ruth and Jo Ann and Shirley are here .Will be here till the 15th of Aug. They have moved to Jacksonville Fla. We are sleeping under a blanket at night. It is really cool enough tonight for a fire. If I didn't have the fireplace cleaned out I would make a fire. Did Frances tell you they are going to put us in some heat? I am so glad for her sake and the baby's.

For this is a cold house. Bruce, tell us as much about yourself as you can for we are glad to know any little things you can tell us.

Your mother and Blanche spent the day with us last week. We enjoyed having them.

We will cable you as soon as the baby arrives which will be a little over two months from now. Dad is well. Will write again sometime. Take care of yourself and come on back as soon as you can. We love you.

Mother Lowrance

(letter #354)

Frances was very excited to hear of the promotion to Lieutenant Colonel.

Envelope marked "Missing!"

July 25, Tuesday (postmark July 26, 1944)

Dearest ex-Major P,

What perfect timing on somebody's account! This has been one more hectic day, and I had just collapsed in the bed feeling quite worn out and unhappy, when the kids came flying back from the post office with the marvelous news that you were a Lt. Colonel! Darling, I must say the first thing I thought was "joy, letter at last" but then I did give proper appreciation to your promotion. In fact you might say I'm "bursting at the seams." (In more ways than one.) After getting your newsy letter I immediately felt better and got up and fixed supper. These are strange powers you have over me, pop! Really I'm as excited about your promotion as I can be. Gosh I will most certainly have to be on my behavior now or you'll demote me! Little P took the news nicely. In fact I think he's a little smug, as if to say , well of course my father has to be more than a mere major!

This expansion business has really got me worried. Nearly two more months yet and well, it just can't be done. Why, I'll never return to size 14 at this rate! Ain't it awful, pop? The family certainly gets a kick out of me and my distresses and now that you're a Col., they think it only fitting that we should have twins, no less. Sometimes I wonder myself.

Had the best intentions of going to the Johnstons tonight but just wasn't up to it. I am going tomorrow morning early though. Surely wish there was some way I could really help them, but only time can do that,

I suppose. Leila and Bob are coming tomorrow so that will be a great help.

Surely wish you could tell me what you're doing and if your present station is permanent. I love you so much. It would be ever so nice to share things with you in person. We've quite a bit of celebrating to catch up on when you come home. Hope your higher rank doesn't require too much dignity! At any rate, I love you just as much and would even give up breakfast in bed if you were here! Don't get into too much trouble, sweetheart. I love you with all my heart (and incidentally am the proudest wife you have ever seen).

Yours always,

Mrs. Lt. Colonel Lulu

(from letter #355)

She wrote again two days later, the same day that Bruce's plane crashed.

Leaders of the 405th Fighter Group, left to right: Col. Bob Delashaw, 405th Fighter Group Commander; Lt. Col. Thornton Mostyn, 405th Executive Officer; Lt. Col. Bruce Parcell, 510th Squadron Commander; Major William Coleman, 511th Squadron Commander; Major Frederick Kinne, kneeling, 509th Squadron Commander. The picture was taken in Picauville during the last week of July, 1944, probably July 25.

Envelope marked "Deceased"

July 27, Thursday (postmark July 28, 1944)

Dearest pop,

I don't expect you to write when you're busy or don't feel in the mood, and I'm not angry with you, although I have missed hear-ing from you. Letters help me quite a lot too. Your recent ones came just at the right time, so that I didn't get depressed. It has been a little hard to keep high spirits since the Johnstons heard about Jim. We try to do all we can for them because they were so nice to Mom and Dad. We haven't been over there any at all today, but Leila and Bob are home now so it really is best to leave them with just the family. They all ask about you and Mr. Johnston is quite proud of your promotion. If you have time, drop them a line because every little bit helps. Do you still get the service letter? I really miss the news.

I love you ever so much, sweetheart. I do hope you're getting my let-ters. Be good now.

Yours only,

Lulu

(from letter #356)

With the news in this next letter, the full impact of the war had started to come home to those with loved ones overseas. Frances talked about a friend named Dave, who was missing. Leonard Fort, a Barium boy and a dear friend, was also missing in action. Although his wife Ruth hoped he had been taken prisoner in Germany, he had in fact been killed in a crash. He had been at-tempting to land his burning plane rather than bail out and ensure the deaths of his crew members. Ruth did not receive official notification of Leonard's death until March of 1945, eight months later.

The remainder of Frances's letters were written after Bruce's death, which would not be officially confirmed until August 27.

Envelope marked "Deceased!" This is crossed through and it is stamped "MISSING."

Dearest Bruce,

I can't get used to writing Col. And I still think it's something I dreamed. I liked the Major pretty well and it seems as if I'm missing a chapter in your life, which is bad. You're my "true love" regardless of rank though.

Spent the morning trying to keep Leila's spirits up, but I think I didn't do much good. This afternoon I went I town to see Lugene. She'd had a telegram that Dave was missing and I also sat a while with Ruth. Leonard is "presumed" missing although there hasn't been any official statement yet. All are just hoping he wasn't the pilot on that mission. I try to control my feelings and not think about it too much, because I know I just must not get upset, but when things hit so close home I can't help but worry a little. I feel about Leonard like he did about Fred, though. If anyone pulls through, he will. I don't ever think about anything happening to you, poppy, mainly because I know you know what you're doing, and too I really have the faith that God will take care of you. If I didn't, I couldn't bear our separation at all. As it is, I miss you so very much. I try to picture you as you are when you write, although I know you're having a lot of hardships. I try to pretend you're seeing the world to tell me and the little one in later years. Look good, pop, and store up a lot of tall tales for us. I can guarantee you a most attentive audience!

We received word this morning that Leonard is missing. I feel quite hopeful that he was just forced down somewhere and will be picked up. Jeff is keeping Ruth so busy she won't have time to think much about it, thank goodness.

The Johnstons are coming over for dinner tonight and there is lots to do so I'll cut this short.

Darling, I love you ever so much. Take good care of yourself.

Always yours,

Lu

(from letter #357)

Envelope marked "Deceased"

July 30 Sun. (postmark July 31, 1944)

Hello poppy,

This day of rest had been anything but, hence I'm writing at a very late hour again. Although I've wanted to write you, it seems these last few weeks I haven't been able to think of anything really important enough to write about. My mind just gets blank. The whole trouble probably is that since I'm not receiving so much mail, I've more or less lost the contact with you that I had when letters came more often.

Ruth feels quite hopeful about Leonard, as do we all. She'd heard through a nurse that the boys lost that day and several days before, were prisoners or else forced down, and there were very few casualties.

It was ever so nice having the Johnstons over last night and I really think they relaxed for a little while. Course I had to show Peggy and Leila my "little things." It's so much fun showing people the things I've made and having them exclaim so. You'd think to hear them that I didn't have brain in my head before I was married!

Had your letter of the 22nd this morning. It's so good to hear from you. I miss you so much, and there just isn't ever any fun without you. Wish I could work up a "hunch" about when you're coming home. If that day ever gets here, I'll be the happiest person alive.

Are you really behaving, with all those pert French girls around? You'd better , or Mrs. P. will be angry! I love you, darling. Please hurry home.

Always,

Lu

(from letter #358)

Frances wrote about Billie Deaton Price, another expectant mother and a friend from Statesville. She was married to Hi Price, who joined the 510th Fighter Squadron at some point following Bruce's death. Billie gave birth to Howard Irving Price III on October 1, 1944. Howard and I were friends throughout our school years in Statesville. I did not know until the 1990s that our fathers had served in the same squadron. Hi and Billie were divorced. He survived the war, remarried, and lived to be eighty-five.

Envelope marked "Deceased"

Aug. 2 Wednesday (postmark August 2, 1944)

Hello sweet pop,

Say, did you know I had a birthday? *(August 1)* I'd forgotten myself until last night. I had been in town nearly all day and when I returned at supper time Mom had a sort of surprise dinner for me with a cake and candles and everything. Dad had made some homemade peach ice cream. It was just luscious. Nina and Lucile were our only special guests. After dinner Billie Deaton invited us up to play bridge. She is expecting a little one in October and we monopolized the conversation with our screwy maternal talk. It was really a very nice birthday, even if I am a year older.

(from letter #360)

Envelope marked "Deceased"

Aug 5, Saturday (postmark August 5, 1944)

Dearest,

The hardest thing for me to do is write when there isn't any mail coming in return. Whatever are they doing to treat me so badly! I'm sure Sunday will bring results though.

If you hear that I have a broken rib, you'll know it was Junior's fault.! Honestly he gets more rambunctious every day! In a way Sept. still seems ever so far away.

In the show last night this couple couldn't agree on a name for the baby, so the child went by "Baby" for three months . Now don't let that happen to us. You never did say what you thought of the two names I selected. I've concluded that Peter Scott Parcell is it unless you've some objections. Do you still dislike Suzan Anne (if it is a girl?) You know your letters are always a month behind so best you let me know these things.

Forgive my dull letters of late, darling, but the mood for writing has passed me by for some reason. I do miss you though, more than ever. Hope things are going well with you.

I love you, Lu

(from letter #361)

Envelope marked "Deceased"

August 6 Sunday (postmark August 7, 1944)

Dearest father P,

I've been reading up on the care and bringing up of the infant also and I'm scared to even think of the great responsibilities. One thing I've made up my mind to is, spoiling or not, I'm going to rock baby to sleep or get in a little "loving" one way or the other. Did you know that little babies sleep twenty out of twenty-four hours? That surely doesn't give me much time to get acquainted and start instructions on father's qualities and looks etc. Guess you'll just have to arrange to come home, Col. P. When I think of all the stuff involved in caring for an infant and the proper ways of doing it, well, I just wonder if I was really cut out for parenthood. Maybe it will be second nature with me by the time you get here!

Most of my stupid chatter is a cover up for my lonesomeness, pop. I thought I'd finally get used to being away from you, but no go. I love you ever so much more today than I did yesterday. That's the way it is every day. Guess you know I couldn't ever care for anyone else. My thoughts are of you and if you don't hurry home, I'm going to do something drastic, like write the war department.

Yours always,

Lu

(from letter # 362)

Envelope marked "Deceased"

Aug. 7, Monday (postmark August 8, 1944)

Dearest Bruce,

Seems like such a long time since I received a letter from you, poppy. Guess I shouldn't complain, but I do miss hearing from you just the same. In fact, when I don't hear I'm quite hard to live with, mainly be-cause I refuse to be "animated," you might say. Things don't interest me in the slightest. Just can't seem to live without you pop.

(from letter #363)

Envelope marked "Deceased"

This was the last letter Frances wrote to Bruce.

Aug. 11 Friday (postmark August 11, 1944)

Dearest,

Have to write to you to get myself in a good mood this morning. Perhaps by the time you've received all those dull letters fussing about no mail, I will have received lots from you so don't take me too seriously when I sound unhappy. I'm a hard lady to live with when your letters don't reach me!

Talked to Ruth Fort yesterday and she seems to think she'll hear something form the other boys in Leonard's squadron by the 25th. Surely hope so because this waiting is enough to get anybody down. I'd planned to go by to see her yesterday after art, but it was too late and my creative exertions were too much for me!

I shouldn't mention this again but are you sure you object to naming the baby Bruce? It's an awfully nice name and it wouldn't be junior. Bet I'm confusing you about the future Parcell's name. I am myself, but at the moment I suppose that's secondary.

I love you, pop. Wish you could only know how much. Remind me to tell you someday. I really miss you so don't tarry there long.

(from letter #365)

This telegram arrived on the morning of August 12, 1944.

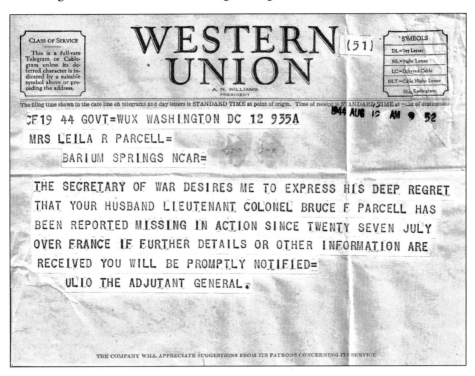

WESTERN UNION (51)

CLASS OF SERVICE

This is a full-rate Telegram or Cablegram unless its deferred character is indicated by a suitable symbol above or preceding the address.

A. N. WILLIAMS
PRESIDENT

SYMBOLS

DL=Day Letter
NL=Night Letter
LC=Deferred Cable
NLT=Cable Night Letter
Ship Radiogram

The filing time shown in the date line on telegrams and day letters is STANDARD TIME at point of origin. Time of receipt is STANDARD TIME at point of destination

CF19 44 GOVT=WUX WASHINGTON DC 12 935A   1944 AUG 12 AM 9 52

MRS LEILA R PARCELL=

    BARIUM SPRINGS NCAR=

THE SECRETARY OF WAR DESIRES ME TO EXPRESS HIS DEEP REGRET THAT YOUR HUSBAND LIEUTENANT COLONEL BRUCE F PARCELL HAS BEEN REPORTED MISSING IN ACTION SINCE TWENTY SEVEN JULY OVER FRANCE IF FURTHER DETAILS OR OTHER INFORMATION ARE RECEIVED YOU WILL BE PROMPTLY NOTIFIED=

    ULIO THE ADJUTANT GENERAL.

THE COMPANY WILL APPRECIATE SUGGESTIONS FROM ITS PATRONS CONCERNING ITS SERVICE

Anne Branan Winslow's letter came as soon as she heard that Bruce was missing.

Saturday (postmark August 12, 1944)

My dearest Lu,

The telegram was the worst possible news. My immediate reaction was to go to you and then I realized this would probably upset you more than anything. Never have I sincerely felt so helpless and wanted to do more. If there were just some way of knowing how best I could serve. My prayers will certainly be that the next news will say that Bruce has landed safely.

I suppose you had just received the notice today when you wired. You can't imagine how deeply I feel and am so thankful that you let me know.

God has His way of dealing with us and naturally we aren't to question why, but there seems to be no sparing in this war. If I could just shoulder some of all this for you. I had just mailed Bruce a letter congratulating him on his colonelcy in which I told him that his Lulu was about the dearest person I knew. I have really found that although you have many friends there is always a time when the one seems the only one and you are that friend to me. I guess that is why the news that Bruce is missing just struck me like a blow. And really, Lu, if you do want me to come, you know you can tell me and I will be there.

When I think of the utter loss of words, I remember that there really is no need to tell those you love how badly you feel.

This event of September becomes even greater now and you must depend a great deal on having a baby. To think that in such a short while you will have gained something unlike any previous experience. Jim and I had planned to map our trip through Barium and I will indeed be looking forward to seeing you. We leave here about Sept. 19th.

Jim joins me in the wish that before many days pass, you will have heard that Bruce is safe. He just has to be!

God bless you. All my love,

Anne

(from letter #367)

The final telegram came one month to the day after Bruce's death, on August 27, 1944.

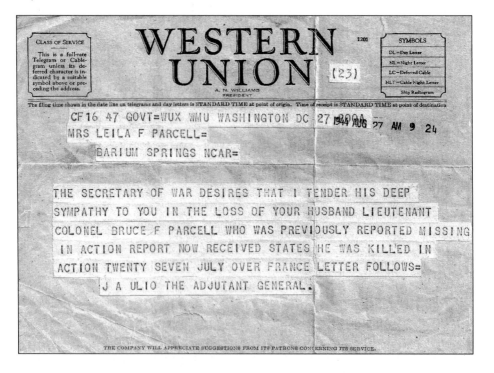

Later Frances would learn from several sources what had happened. On July 27 Bruce was flying an armed reconnaissance mission near Coutances when his P-47 Thunderbolt, the Little Lulu, was hit by flak at 1,500 feet. He dove to avoid being hit again, and was not able to gain altitude after that. The plane plummeted to the ground and exploded. Bailing out was not an option at such a low altitude. On the very next day General George Patton's big break-through of the German lines at St. Lo began. Germans were retreating south-ward away from the front lines. On that day, under the orders of the 510th Squadron's new commander Ralph Jenkins, the pilots destroyed seventy-six trucks, three armored cars, sixteen horse-drawn vehicles, four half trucks, and one small car. Bombing in the immediate aftermath of Bruce's death was so fierce that the squadron received a commendation for their "aggressive spirit and skillful manner in which these missions were accomplished." The 509th and 511th also flew numerous successful missions on July 28. On July 29 the 405th Fighter Group was cited by the Ninth Air Force as the "outstanding group of the day" for missions of the previous day. Revenge certainly played a part in this accolade.

In the year 2000 a Frenchman named Remy Chuinard published a book called *A Stormy Sky Over Normandy : Summer 1944*. In it he tried to portray the heroism of the young American pilots who flew the single-seat fighter bombers and the ground crews who supported them. To illustrate the role of the fighter-bombers, he devoted an entire chapter to the exploits of the 510th Squadron during the summer of 1944. I believe that my mother never fully understood the exact circumstances of my father's death. Maybe it was more than she could bear to think about. She certainly never attempted to share any details with me. Chuinard wrote an explicit account of what happened that day. His sources came from interviews with surviving pilots and others who were involved in the war. He refers to Bruce as a Major, but Bruce's letters clearly show that he was promoted to Lieutenant Colonel, effective July 6.

In the book, Chuinard told of 1,503 heavy bombers in the sky from St. Lo to Coutances. They were escorted by 500 fighter planes and planned to drop 3,400 tons of bombs on the area that day. As Bruce was flying low to avoid ground fire, the Little Lulu was hit and Bruce radioed in, "I'm hit…I'm hit… I'm going down." Because he was only about sixty feet above ground at this point, his parachute was useless. According to his wing man Charles Appel, who witnessed the whole event, Bruce climbed onto the wing of his plane. Then there was a crash and a huge explosion.

While this is a somewhat accurate account of events, others knew additional details about Bruce's crash. Bill Smith, an enlisted man from Spencer, North Carolina, who knew Bruce overseas, told my mother and me the story of his attempting to open his parachute while he stood on the wing of the plane. Pilots were trained to do this in the hope that, at such a low altitude, the parachute might catch wind and pull them away from the crashing plane. In any case, this did not work and Bruce died in the ensuing explosion.

Condolence letters began to arrive almost immediately after the news of Bruce's death was received. Wilson and Frances, aka Skinny and Frankie, wrote as soon as they heard.

Sunday night (postmark August 28, 1944)

Dear Frances,

We got Dad's telegram this afternoon and were distressed to hear the sad news about Bruce. We have been hoping and praying that he was alright. It's hard to believe that war can be so terrible. It is impossible to express how sorry we are. You know what I have always thought of Bruce. Although I only saw him one time after you all were married, I will never forget the years we were in high school and college together. Bruce was clean in body and spirit and a gentleman in every respect. I feel that I am a better man by having known and lived with him.

Now you will have to pattern your future in the way that Bruce would want you to if he were able to direct it. You not only have your life to live but soon there will be another life, either little "Bruce" or little "Lu", which you will have to direct. It will be a full time job to do it right and I know you will do a good job of it. You are young and life will adjust itself in time. Put your trust in God and you will find that life comes much easier.

Frances, keep your chin up because Bruce would want you to do that and think of the important job you have ahead of you. You owe it to Bruce and Fred and all the others who have made the supreme sacrifice to carry on and to make this a better world for our children to live in.

Love,

Wilson

Appended to the bottom of Skinny's letter was this.

Dear Frances:

We were so distressed and shocked when we got Mr. Lowrance's telegram. You know that you have our sincere sympathy and if there is ever anything we can do please let us know. We feel so helpless.

Our thoughts and prayers are with you. Love, Frances *(Frankie)*

This letter was from Dr. Jim Winslow, Anne's husband. Jim had great affection for my mother.

Tuesday AM (postmark August 30, 1944)

Dear Lu,

I was delivering a first child tonight and had wondered a little about how yours would be, when Ann called. For the rest of the night I've been wondering if I have anything worth saying. My sympathy would be a hollow little thing, for I know the way you loved him. You alone can realize the loss. Please remember when you can that Ann and I and those like us are wishing you all possible strength, as each of us realize our loss.

It's quiet in early morning here, but in places it isn't quiet, men are risking and giving life for one thing, their principles. It's not for patriotism or wealth, or democracy or to protect their own lives that they risk them. It's for their souls, their individual thoughts and convictions, that they fight. Living would be blank without such a burning core. We are a part of a long chain; we have been given this priceless thing by past generations, and we have lived when we have passed it on. I believe that is the conduct of man, Lu, and their children have a rich heritage.

This little I wanted to say. All the rest, Lu, I know you understand better than I could write.

Yours, J

Leila Johnston wrote eloquently not long after learning of the death of her own brother Jim in the war.

September 7, 1944

Dearest Frances,

Almost exactly five years ago the war in Europe began; at that time you were ready to begin your Junior year at Queens and I my Sophomore year at Salem. And although the thought of war seemed terrible to us even then, yet little did we dream that we would be faced with the immense personal tragedies we have suffered. Who would have imagined that our generation should be called upon to sacrifice so much?

You'll never know how much you have been in my thoughts, Frances, and many times I have tried to write, but each attempt would end in a miserable heap of crumpled paper and even now I can't say much, except to let you know that I'm sharing your grief and wish there were something I could really do to help.

Leila Johnston

Mother writes that you are being marvelously brave, and that's what all who know you would expect you to be. There's nothing to do but try to be brave, thanking God for the wonderful memories of two years spent with one you loved, memories that will always stay as young and loving as you two were. You can be grateful that he was a fine, modest, strong, gentlemanly young Christian with many friends who are better for having known him. And we can hold on to the faith that some good must come out of this, if we set our minds and wills toward that end.

When someone like Bruce is killed, one wonders how the world—as well as those who loved him—will get on without him. It's a lifetime job for all of us, living so that in a small way the loss will have compensation.

Whenever you want to write exactly how you feel, no matter how blue, write me and I'll understand. Wish I could be at home now to talk to you.

Lots of love,

Leila

(letter #371)

Frances was grieving but she had another concern to occupy her thoughts. Her due date was September 27, and she had to be prepared for my birth. Unlike Frances and Bruce, the Winslows were always hoping for a girl. I was born on the afternoon of September 24, 1944. After months of discussion of possible names in their letters, in which my father stated quite clearly his dislike of his own name, she named me Bruce!

Bruce Anne Parcell

September 24, 1944

Lt. Col. and Mrs. Bruce Fraley Parcell

This letter followed soon after. Anne often referred to Frances as Ludie, her own version of Mother's nickname. The Winslows must have just visited Frances in Barium Springs the day before.

Brooklyn, N.Y. Sept. 26, 1944

Dearest Mother P.—

May we express our greatest delight over our new niece? To think my Ludie has a little girl—why it's marvelous. I do hope she looks just like you.

But why didn't you have her twenty-four hours earlier? You never can tell about Miss Bruce Anne Parcell, can you?

We called in to the hotel before coming out and the clerk said we had a telegram. Jim flew out to the car grinning from ear to ear, mumbling, "hope it's a girl." So we could hardly wait to get here and see! I am so anxious to know all about her. Does she have any hair, blue eyes, cupid's bow lips, etc? Won't we dress her up though? I can't decide whether she should go to Vassar or Sweetbriar. And how will we ever decide on Chi O or ADII. After all, she's half mine. Doesn't she bear my name? I just don't see how I can wait very long to see her. Make them take good care of you and you take care of "little P."

All our love,

Annie the Aunt

(from letter #372)

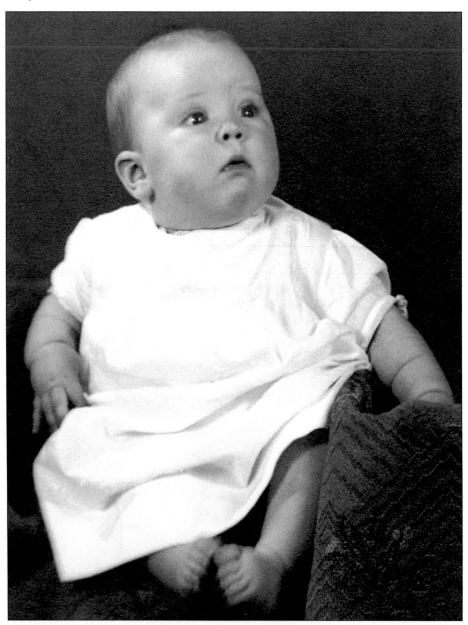

Here I am, Bruce Anne Parcell, the long-awaited blessed event, but not a boy after all. Still, I received a boy's name.

Leila Johnston also wrote to express congratulations, but not to Frances. Here is the first letter ever addressed to me.

United States Naval Air Station, Jacksonville, Florida

September 29, 1944

Dearest Bruce Ann,

Among all the inconveniences of this day and time, there are several that have irritated me exceedingly the past few weeks. The first is that I couldn't be at Barium to be among those to have a first glimpse of you, for all of us have waited long and earnestly for your arrival; the second is that flowery telegrams are taboo, for I had an especially blossomy one all made up for you! But conditions being what they are, and you being who you are, I am sure that you will understand the reason for these things and will overlook them.

Leila Johnston

Little girl, you can never know how all the grandparents, aunts, uncles, cousins, and friends are thrilled to know that at last you are here, and all of us want to extend you a hearty welcome. Hurry up and feel right at home, and among other things you want to do right away is to put your feet in your mouth, because it saves washing and helps to make both ends meet. (My conscience tells me to admit that the last idea wasn't original.)

I am glad that you are a little girl, Bruce Ann, because then you will have a chance to grow up to be like your Mother. Of course, that's aiming for the stars, but you're one who can do it, with the Mother to help. And remember that here's one who will be pulling for you all the way and expecting great things of you.

Lots of love, little girl.

Leila

Harry Gillett was Bruce's roommate from his time in California and best man in their wedding. In the days following my birth, many other condolence letters arrived.

Sept. 28, 1944 (postmark September 30, 1944)

Dear Lu,

I kept putting off writing until I was sure I could write in words how I felt about the bad news of Bruce. Reading it in your letter was quite a shock and it seemed almost impossible to be true. Bruce was the closest friend I ever had, he was a brother to me, and my only wish is that we could have spent more time together. Bruce was looked up to and respected by all that knew him, there is no doubt of him being a superior officer at all times.

Lu, I wish you could tell me more about how it all happened. Was Bruce flying out of England or down our way in Italy when he went over? If it was in Italy it makes me feel worse, if possible, to know that we were so close together and unable to make contact.

Tony and I have been wondering if you have had your baby yet. We do hope you will let us know when it arrives.

I'm going to an instructor's school here and when I finish it to go to my next station, Tony and I hope we will be able to come by and see you.

This is all for now, Lu, hoping to hear from you and your baby soon.

Harry

P.S. Please send me Bruce's mother's address. Tell your mother and father hello for me.

(letter #373)

Sandy Johnston was a good friend in the military. His wife was also named Frances. He painted a very different picture of the war from what Bruce had been writing home about. His account of the plane crash, while not first-hand, sounds authentic.

Oct. 14 (postmark Oct. 16, 1944)

Dear Lu,

I'm not much at writing this sort of letter, particularly since I'm one of the most fortunate chaps who's back, but Frances told me you've been quite naturally wanting to get in touch with one of us, and I'd of course written you much sooner if it had been permitted.

Needless to say, things were mighty rough for quite a while before D-day and once we got to France it was a case of losing planes and pilots about every time we went out. The Jerries *(Germans)*, at that time, were not yet on the run, and we were doing nothing but ground strafing and dive bombing on targets called in to us by the ground forces. There weren't any easy ones, no matter where we went behind the lines. They were throwing one proverbial kitchen sink at us no matter what altitude we flew.

The last day I flew with Bruce, the brass sent us after some bridges on the Vire River near St. Lo. It took us three straight missions to knock out one, and cost us four pilots in the process. Bruce and I flew in the same section (we had the squadron split in two, each flying noon to noon) and that day it was his bombs that got one bridge.

A few days later I got a five day leave back in England, so I wasn't with him when he went down.

Hell, Lu, I'm not going to try to tell you what he was like, you were married to him. But I'm damned if I've ever admired, respected, and thought more of him as a chap or as a squadron C.O. than when we were in France. He was really on top of the world, tickled as the devil over your kid being on the way, damn pleased over his promotion, and full of the sort of confidence a guy gets when he's doing the toughest sort of job under the worst conditions, and damn well knows he's doing it right from any angle. I know you're proud of him, and you sure have every right to be.

When the allied lines moved up later, he and another boy were found, and they were both buried in an American military place pretty close by. I'm sure I could find the name of the town if you'd like to know.

It was of course ground fire that caught Bruce, but from all I could make out, talking with the chaps who were flying, he must have been instantaneously killed. I hate writing like this to you, but from what Frances and my parents have said at one time or another, it's likely you'd prefer to know than to wonder. We were always operating close to the ground though, and it couldn't have been anything but a split second affair.

As for us, as one of four in the 510th at Walterboro who didn't get shot down, I've a damn good idea how very lucky I am. And it held straight on thru, for I got here the afternoon of the 9th, and our daughter Alexandra Winans J. (8 lbs. 9 oz.) was born the morning of the 10th, and both in the finest of health now. Needless to say, I sure was glad to hear about Bruce Ann.

Look, Lu, as I've said, I sure don't go much for this writing business, but if there's anything I could tell you or do for you, I sure wish you'd drop me a line at this address.

Next month I might be passing by on the way to a new base, and if I could tell you anything, I'd be glad to. I'd sure give you all my sympathy if I thought you were the type who wanted it.

We were all in one damn tough setup and we all knew it would be only the few very lucky ones who got thru it time after time. Skill as a pilot didn't have anything to do with it, just plain good or bad luck with no rhyme nor reason to it. And it's the ones like you who have to take it as a result. Sure is hard to make much sense out of it. I can't anyhow.

Anyhow, please don't hesitate to let me know if there's anything at all I can do. Frances is writing you soon and we'd both like to keep in touch with you and the nipper.

Best regards, Sandy

(from letter #374)

Ralph Jenkins became squadron commander after Bruce was killed. Again, he described the war as it really was. Bruce had gone to great lengths to protect Frances from that reality. The breakthrough that he mentions was what allowed General George Patton's Third Army to break out of the Normandy beach heads and start the long allied march towards Germany.

112 West 8th Ave., Tallahassee, Florida, Nov. 23, 1944
(postmark November 24, 1944)

Dear Lu,

Ever since Bruce was shot down last July I have wanted to write to you but because of Army regulations I couldn't then write what I wanted to say. Col. Delashaw and many of the boys of the Group are home now and I suppose that you have heard the story of your husband's death. I imagine that you'll want to hear my version of the story, for it should make you very proud.

It was during the most active period of air warfare in Normandy. The operation ending in the now famous breakthrough to the very gates

Ralph Jenkins receiving the Distinguished Flying Cross, probably sometime in late 1944.

of Germany was very actively engaged in by Bruce's squadron. Ours was the task to operate over the very hazardous zone just in back of the front lines. In the enemy rear zone were bridges that had to be blown into the river and there were enemy supply columns bringing up reinforcements to try to counteract that offensive at St. Lo. All of these targets were heavily defended by anti-aircraft guns. In the preceding days our squadron had outstanding successes in destroying the enemy although it had cost us several pilots. In spite of the growing opposition and resultant danger, Bruce continued to lead his squadron with the same determination to destroy everything German. For this display of courage and splendid leadership, Bruce won the affection and admiration of all in the squadron. Even though there are no Walterboro boys left, he will never be forgotten in his 510th.

It was during one of these missions that Col. Parcell was caught in a screen of enemy ack-ack. Being at such a low altitude while strafing, he could not bail out and unable to find a suitable landing spot, had to crash land. If you saw the movie "A Guy Named Joe" you'll know why there is nothing more to be said.

Bruce's body was recovered just a few days later as the whole operation was a success and the Germans swept out.

Several of we pilots and a few enlisted men, all who admired your husband so much, attended his funeral at an American Military Cemetery on the coast near the invasion beaches. Our chaplain Lanholt officiated. About all I want to say is that Bruce along with many other of his squadron mates gave his life for his country, dying for a righteous cause. Though their contributions while flying were great, their greatest will always be in having left the model of courage and daring for the squadron. This spirit to win will be with us until victory is won.

Sincerely yours,

Ralph C. Jenkins

Tiero *(Ralph's wife)* joins me in sending our congratulations on the arrival of Bruce Ann. We're going to send something shortly.

While condolence letters were pouring in, Frances also received an official letter from a Captain in the Ninth Air Force to tell her that Bruce was being posthumously awarded the Distinguished Flying Cross. His name was Forest B. Stith. Interestingly, this was the same man who wrote "Deceased" on Bruce's last letter to Frances. The letter is on the facing page.

In February of 1945 Frances received a letter from D.B. Segars. He was the McBee high school student who put the poison ivy vine on Frances's desk in hopes that she would not leave her teaching job to get married.

At work Fri. Nite (postmark February 24, 1945)

Dear Mrs. Parcell,

Just a few lines as I have a few extra minutes to spare. I was sitting here wondering who I could write a letter to and I happened to think about you. I wrote to Mr. and Mrs. Frick quite a while ago and received a letter from them giving me this address, so I thought that I would try and write and see if you receive it; be sure and answer so I will know that you received it.

In Mrs. Frick's letter, she told me about your husband and brother getting killed in action. I wish to extend my deepest sympathy, and my deepest heartfelt thoughts go out to you and your family.

I know you remember me, without my reminding you. Yes, believe it or not it is that mean little Segars boy writing to you. I have grown quite a bit since I was in your class though. Do you remember the time that you gave me a broom and told me to sweep the Home Ec. Room, and I took the stick end and went scraping across the floor? I also remem-

HEADQUARTERS
NINTH AIR FORCE

APO 696, U S Army
13 November 1944.

GENERAL ORDERS)
    :
NUMBER.....267)

*   *   *

SECTION III

1. By direction of the President, under the provisions of the Act of Congress approved 2 July 1926 (Bull 8, WD, 1926), and in accordance with authority delegated by the War Department a DISTINGUISHED FLYING CROSS is awarded to the following-named officers and enlisted man:

BRUCE F. PARCELL, O-370357, Lieutenant Colonel, 405th Fighter Group. For extraordinary achievement while participating in aerial flight against the enemy in the European Theater of Operations. Throughout a most important phase of the Air Offensive, Europe, and the Normandy Campaign Lt Col PARCELL distinguished himself by conspicuous gallantry, leadership, and fearless flying technique in leading his squadron in difficult and arduous attacks against the enemy transportation facilities and in the course of numerous important missions in direct support of the ground forces in operations on the Continent. His unusual leadership was instrumental in the success which attended the operations of his organization, and his deep devotion to duty is in keeping with the highest traditions of the Service. This award is made posthumously. Next of Kin: Mrs. Leila F. Parcell (Wife), Barium Springs, North Carolina.

*   *   *

By command of Major General VANDENBERG:

W W MILLARD
Col G S C
C of S

OFFICIAL:

/s/ C M Seebach
/t/ C M SEEBACH
  Colonel AGD
  Adj General

DISTRIBUTION: "A"

A TRUE EXTRACT COPY:

FOREST B. STITH,
Captain, Air Corps.

207

ber the time that we had to make a speech as to why we didn't like the study hall, those were some speeches.

Mrs. Parcell, I know you remember my sister, Juanita, at least I don't think that you could forget her because she was much more mischievous than I was. Well she got married about 4 months after she finished school. She has a little boy eight months old. He certainly does get around too. He can't even sit alone yet, but he has been in the hospital two or three times since he was born. She calls him "Pee Wee." That is a cute name for a baby, but it won't suit him when he gets grown.

I am working in the Charleston Navy yard, doing clerical work, and I like it just fine, excepting that I'm on the night shift right now. I go to work at 5:45 in the afternoon and get off at 3:30 in the morning. Those aren't such satisfying hours, are they? I have been working here for 19 months.

I wanted to go to work on the outside, but I had to take an office job. I don't think you taught school in McBee the last year I went, but anyway 19 days before I graduated I was in an automobile wreck and broke every bone in my right arm, through the elbow. It has left my right arm crooked, and a partial paralysis. Three of my fingers are completely paralyzed. I sure did have some bad luck. I guess you can tell there is something wrong with my arm by the way I type. It really does hurt me at sometimes, but at others it doesn't hurt so much.

I guess that you are tired of reading my gossip, so I guess it is about time to bring this letter to a close, so please write to me real soon, and let me know how you are getting along. Nita said to tell you hello. She lives about 4 doors from us.

Be good, and write to me as soon as you get this. I will be looking forward to an answer. My mother did live here but she has moved back to McBee.

Please excuse all these mistakes, but I hope that you will understand, as I have told you that my arm is partly paralyzed. Write me, and send me a picture of yourself if you have one, as Nita and I both would love to see you.

As Ever,

A Pupil (Formerly)

D.B.

(letter #376)

The chaplain of the 405th Fighter Group wrote a letter to Frances on August 15, 1944, shortly after the confirmation of Bruce's death. Unfortunately she did not receive it until March of 1945.

My dear Leila *(Frances's first name)*:

It is utterly impossible for me to express in words the sorrow which overwhelmed the entire Group when the news of Bruce's death reached us. We were simply stunned, and still are, for Bruce was not only a friend in the deepest sense of the word, but a leader of his men, respected for his sterling character, loved and honored for his example of high and decent living. We have lost much in the Group, and our sorrow is deep.

But Leila, our loss, great as it is, is as nothing compared to yours. The close fellowship of the men has given us a knowledge of each other, of the hopes and plans and dreams. We knew about you and the event you were expecting, and our hearts are doubly torn as we think of it. The men who have been together now for a long time, and who had the privilege of knowing you both back in Florida and South Carolina often talk of you and Bruce, and I wish there were some way of letting you know the genuine and heartfelt sympathy of those men.

Bob was overcome, for he and Bruce have been together a long time. He will probably write to you later on, but just now I speak for all the men who cannot write at this time, and would try by these feeble words to let you know what our hearts are attempting to say to you.

On August 11th, a group of his friends went with me to the American Cemetery where Bruce was buried, and held a simple service. I read parts of John 14, and the 15th, 23rd, and 121st Psalms: there was a prayer, and a benediction; and then the Military Honors. The little service, quiet, impressive, simple, was fitting for a man, loved for his upright and decent life.

It is our continuing prayer that God shall bless you with the peace and comfort which only He can give in times like this.

On the Sunday preceding his death, Bruce was in Church in the Squadron area. He always came when duties permitted, and I am glad that he was able to be there on that Sunday. I talked with him just before his last mission, and he told me how eager he was looking forward to hearing about the great event back home. And then he went--just as he would have chosen had he been given the choice--performing his duty in the face of the enemy, giving his full measure of devotion to make this a better world for all men.

We are most anxious about you, for we know what you are going through. We hope that everything will be alright, and I trust that you may be aware of the prayers and well wishes of your many friends here. It would be better could we write personal letters to you but this is war, and we must obey the regulations. We hope you will understand.

I am sure that Bruce's old friends here in the group will call on you after this is over. I hope to be able to do so too. In the meantime, you will receive instructions from the government on the insurance and other benefits, and will be told at some future date about the removal of Bruce's remains to the States after the hostilities cease. His personal effects have been gathered together and will be sent on to you later.

We have done all that we could do. The example of Bruce's leadership, of his outstanding character, and of his sacrifice in giving all, will gird us on to greater effort, and help make of us all something of the man he was.

May God bless you and yours in this hour of sorrow and grief.

Sincerely yours,

Frank J. Landolt, Chaplain

Mother talked to me about my birth but never much about how she dealt with my father's death. However, she did share her feelings in her autobiography. She wrote of that sad time, "My parents, my friends, everyone kept saying, 'Don't cry,' 'Be brave,' 'After all you are going to have a baby and it's not good for the baby to be too emotional.' Day after day it became harder and harder to accept my husband's death even though I was carrying his child. I just wanted the world to end so we could be together again." But once I was actually here, she began to heal because she had to. Babies need a lot of attention.

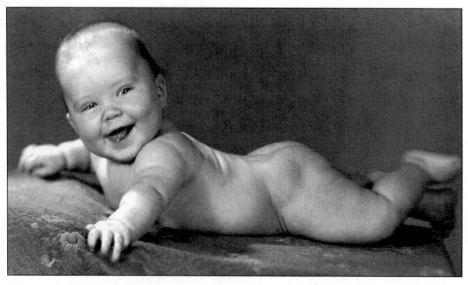

But having a baby did not prevent her from undertaking a long trip when I was about ten months old. Her friend Anne, who could always talk her into almost anything, asked her to drive across country to meet up with Anne's husband Jim, who was in the Navy as a medical officer. So off they went, sometime during the summer of 1945. I was left with my aunt Ruth in Jacksonville, Florida. Existing telegrams from that time period are all dated in August, so possibly the war was over by the time they left home. They saw many sights, including New Orleans, the Sonoran Desert, San Clemente, San

Frances with Anne Winslow

At my aunt Ruth's home in Jacksonville, Florida, early September, 1945. Mother and I are getting to know each other again after her trip out west.

211

Francisco, the Grand Canyon and Yellowstone National Park. They returned home sometime in September. Ruth wired the following to Mother on September 3:

> BRUCE IS WELL AND HAPPY EVERYONE IS FINE GLAD YOU ARE HEADED HOME DONT EXPECT BRUCE TO RECOGNIZE YOU=RUTH.

This proved prophetic, for Mother told me that in fact I did not know who she was when she returned. We had to get acquainted all over again.

Shortly after her return home, Mother was invited to go to Greensboro, North Carolina, to the Overseas Replacement Depot to accept the posthumously awarded Distinguished Flying Cross for my father. She agreed with the stipulation that the award would be pinned on me. I was one year old. She loved telling the story of how the presiding Colonel took me in his arms, whereupon I wet on him. The event (awarding, not wetting), is preserved in a newspaper clipping describing the ceremony.

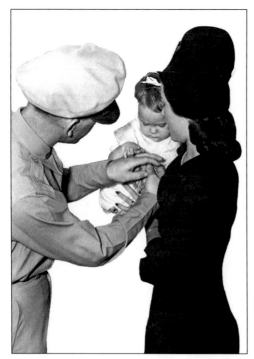 

Here I am, age one, receiving the posthumously awarded Distinguished Flying Cross.

Few letters are available for the next several months. Then, in March of 1946, Mother wrote home from Jacksonville, where she seems to have been babysitting for Ruth's daughters, Jo Ann and Shirley. Ruth's husband was Joe Rhyne. It was 1946, and I would have been eighteen months old. When I was that age, I was apparently still called Bruce, instead of Bruce Anne, which sounds very odd to me now.

Monday morning (postmark March 7, 1946)

Dearest family,

Bruce and I are out taking a sunbath. Rather, I am--she's wandering around visiting the chickens and the neighbors. Her cold is all gone and we're all fit as a fiddle.

Ruth and Joe are in Des Moines but I don't know when they'll be home. Ruth says Joe has been quite successful in getting grain so I suppose they'll be back sometime this week.

Bruce helps me wash the dishes every morning and also the clothes. She really thinks she's something. The minute breakfast is over she pulls her chair up to the sink and says "Wash the dishes" and when she finishes she says "wash your hands."

She's improving on the training business and eats almost entirely by herself now. She's cutting six teeth but is real good considering. They're just about thru now, thank goodness.

Jo Ann went to her party at the church Friday night. She looked real nice in Ruth's dress and had a nice time. Shirley and another little girl are going to sing in some sort of talent show at school and she's been practicing like she was going to sing over the radio. We're getting along just fine. Bruce goes to the grocery store with me and has the best time.

I won't say about coming home till Ruth comes home.

Love to you all,

Frances and Bruce Anne

(from letter #377)

In April of 1946 another letter from Chaplain Landolt arrived. Here are some excerpts.

My dear Mrs. Parcell,

Bruce was buried in LaCambe Cemetery (near Isigny and Carenton) on the Normandy Peninsula, Section AC row 2 grave 30. I told you about the service in my letter of the 15th of August 1944 (which I have recently discovered you did not get until March of 1945). Later Bruce's

July 31st 1944. On the foreground, Bruce Parcell's grave, in the temporary American cemetery of La Cambe.

sister sent for information, but I could not answer that letter myself according to regulations…many times I wish that I had just thrown all regulations to the wind, and written the full story.

LaCambe Cemetery is a very lovely and beautiful spot. It is located on the main Cherbourg-Paris Road, and is about one mile from the beach where the landings were made on June 6, 1944.

The St. Lo attack by air took place in the morning *(of July 27, 1944)* at 11:00 AM. That afternoon, Bruce flew an armed reconnaissance mission, on which he was killed. I told you in my letter last year that I talked with him just before the mission. He was coming out of the intelligence trailer, and had on his flying equipment. He had a few minutes, so we stood by the steps, and chatted. It was then he told me about you, and how anxious he was about the coming baby. Personally I doubt if he had any "social" conversation after that, for he went immediately to the line, and from then on it was business only. The news which we had a very short time later was indeed a blow to me in view of the above incident.

Your loss has been so great. May God bless you and yours richly with His comfort and peace. With kindest personal greetings, I am,

Very truly yours,

Frank J. Landolt

In an ironic twist, today La Cambe is a cemetery for German soldiers killed in France in World War II. It is indeed a beautiful spot, now filled with small black crosses and a large Germanic-looking monument.

Killed In Action

Once again that dred telegram expressing the sympathy of the Secretary of War over the death of a soldier has been received at

LT. COLONEL BRUCE PARCELL

Barium, this time for Lt. Colonel Bruce Parcell, killed in action over France on July 27th.

Just a week before his wife received a telegram stating that he was missing in action. He was the pilot of a fighter plane, and his squadron was extremely busy during the latter part of July making possible the breakthrough of Patton's army. Every news broadcast had something to say of the effectiveness of the fighter command in the part they played in this tremendous thing. This effort was costly, and the life of this fine young man was part of the price paid in this effort.

Bruce came to Barium as an eleven year old boy on the 27th of August, 1928. He was a good student, a serious minded, friendly youngster. One of the jobs that he had as a lad was minding the sheep Maybe he, like David of old, had time to think a lot of things out while the sheep were on their good behavior. Surely many things that he did and said in his later life bore out the fact that he thought more deeply of many things than the average boy. He graduated from Barium in 1934 and immediately went to Davidson College where he graduated in 1938. That same year he entered the army; this was long before Pearl Harbor. Bruce entered the Air Corps and later became a pilot.

His rating when he entered the army was 2nd Lieutenant. When he met his death in 1944, he was a Lt. Colonel, an average of an advancement of one rank a year.

He saw much service in this country; he rated tops as an instructor. He was careful of his men and during the latter part of his stay in the states, he was instructor in squadron maneuvers.

In March, 1944, he went to England and immediately began to see active combat. During his service he was awarded the Air Medal and Four Oak Leaf Clusters.

Many of the boys from Barium Springs are in the Air Corps. Some are navigators, mechanics, bombardiers, pilots. Bruce was the only one who piloted a fighter plane. We have heard him express satisfaction over this. He said when he

Killed In Action

(Continued From Page One)

went into battle, he did not want to feel responsible for other lives than his own, that the responsibility of leading a squadron is enough without feeling that an error in judgment or a mechanical failure might cause him to be even slightly responsible for the lives of other members of his crew.

We can imagine this lad in his last battle as a brave leader, hunting out danger spots himself and protecting the other ships of his squadron whenever possible - surely a noble leader of men!

While we at Barium will never again see his face, we will cherish in our memory the high ideals and the brave deeds of this fine young man.

Bruce's mother lives at Cleveland, North Carolina. His widow and her parents live at Barium. Bruce had two sisters younger than he at Barium, two older than he who never came to Barium. These older sisters helped Bruce with his education, and he most generously helped his younger sisters with theirs. Surely we must all be better men and women for having accepted for our protection the life of this young man.

POSTWAR LIFE

The chaplain's was the last of the letters saved from the 1940s. So ends the story of my parents' life together. Mother would go on to get several part-time jobs, including teaching dietetics at a Statesville hospital, serving briefly as food service director for the orphanage, and teaching for a year at Barium Springs High School. She then took a full time job with the Iredell County Extension Service in Statesville as an Assistant Home Demonstration Agent and 4-H advisor. We continued to live with my grandparents in Barium Springs and my grandmother took care of me during the day.

Frances with her colleague and friend Iris Sowers at Iredell County Extension Service.

Mother eventually began dating two men at the same time. One was a former Barium boy, A.D. Potter, who had started a successful manufacturing plant that made ladies' lingerie. He was very interested in marrying her.

Left to right: A.D. Potter, Frances's one-time serious boy friend; Frances; Jim and Anne Winslow.

The other man was Rowe McNeely, the man she would marry in June of 1950 when I was five years old. She had met Rowe through work, as he was an Assistant County Agent for the Iredell County Extension Service. Even though this was a second marriage for both of them *(Rowe's first wife Lurleen had died of cancer)*, the wedding was again a fairly elaborate affair. I was the flower girl and Leila Johnston played the piano. The ceremony took place at my grandparents' home in Barium Springs. The tall staircase served as the main aisle that Mother and I descended. I wore a pale green floor-length dress that was hand-made by my grandmother. My naturally curly hair hung down in ringlets, and I felt very grown up to be participating in this important event.

Frances at Myrtle Beach on a trip with A.D. I went along as the chaperone.

Mother and Rowe, whom I would someday decide to call Daddy like my half-sisters and brother did, went off on a honeymoon to Niagara Falls. I was left behind with my grandparents, but I received postcards and little gifts while they were away. Upon their return, we moved into a small duplex in Statesville while our new house was being built. We moved into that house at 870 Henkel Road when I was in first grade and lived there until I graduated from high school in 1962.

My sister Jane was born in 1951, Rowena in 1954, and brother Chris in 1958 when I was thirteen years old and in the eighth grade. During those child

Rowe and Frances, on a date before they were married.

rearing years, Mother served as president of the Junior Service League. She headed the League's successful campaign for a bond issue to build a recreation center and swimming pool in Statesville and also championed the addition of fluoride to Statesville's water supply, a cause which succeeded with her enthusiastic support.

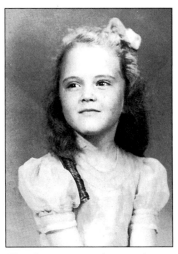

Here I am in my pale green dress in June, 1950.

I tell this part of Mother's life story to illustrate just how strong and determined a person she was and how she was able to overcome her grief to remake her life. But grief continued to follow her. Rowe would die of cancer in 1979. In 1985 my sister Jane would also die of cancer at the age of thirty-four. So Frances, aka Lu, suffered much sadness in her life. This did not dim her enthusiasm for living, however. In 1969 she took a job in the Food Service Department of Rowan Memorial Hospital in Salisbury, North Carolina, a position she would hold until 1987. During those years she gained the admiration and respect of everyone she worked with. Then came retirement and a chance to travel, which she took up with a vengeance. She went on a safari tour of Kenya and came away hooked on world travel. In subsequent years she, along with her still-best friend Anne and Anne's husband Jim, traveled to such places as Portugal, India, Pakistan, the Persian Gulf, and South Africa.

But there is more to the story yet. As the years went by, I grew up with a sense that I was different and set apart. All of my friends had two biological parents, while I had only one. I had a grandmother and aunts and cousins that were not related to anyone else in my immediate family. And I had this strange boy's name that I kept having to explain. I felt compelled to tell complete strangers that I was named for my father because he had died in the war, without ever fully comprehending what that meant. I did not know the full story. Plus my last name was Parcell, while the rest of my family mem-

Anne Branan Winslow and Frances, who was only ever called Lu by Anne, at Frances's home in Salisbury, N.C., sometime in the 1990s.

bers were McNeelys. There was always a lot of explaining to do. It was just not quite normal. I survived all that, although even to this day I have problems with my name. Often people think I am saying Ruth Ann, or that I am giving them my husband's name instead of my own. Mother never understood what a problem this was. She thought my name was beautiful. I guess she had forgotten that my father had strenuously objected to both Bruce and Anne.

Over the years Mother received a few invitations to attend reunions of the 405th Fighter Group. She had long been out of touch with her old friends from the Air Corps. In 1984 Ralph Jenkins, in an effort to locate Mother, had written to the mayor of Cleveland, N.C. He hoped that the mayor might know the whereabouts of Bruce's surviving kin. The mayor's name was Bill Allison and as it happened, he had been Director of Food Service at Rowan Memorial Hospital in Salisbury where Mother worked as his assistant. (She became the Director when he retired in 1981). Mr. Allison gave Ralph her address, which is how she came to receive the invitations. At last, in 1998, she decided to attend the next reunion. It was to take place in Orlando, Florida, and my Aunt Sarah Parcell Howard and her husband Bill were going too. Mother invited me to go along. It was a fun experience, and I was able to meet Ralph and his wife Tiero, Bob Delashaw and his wife Cile, plus many other people whose names I did not quite absorb. The men were clearly happy for us to be there, but I really did not get too many stories about my father. In Mother's files I found drafts of thank-you letters to the Delashaws and the Jenkins family, but I am not sure if she ever mailed anything to them. Here they are in her notes format.

Bob and Cile,

There's a song called "Feelings" that certainly expresses what Bruce Anne and I felt during the Orlando weekend. To pick up friendships instantly after such a long space of absence was not only remarkable but so gratifying.

There are always regrets about becoming lax in our associations with friends, but memories are wonderful and our recent weekend with the "group" has added an unforgettable addition.

Thank you for the pictures and also the book on the 405th. There is so much that those of us at home didn't realize--perhaps just as well.

Reliving the past makes me very eager to keep in touch so please let's not wait for Chicago. Living alone gives me lots of room for company and I'm issuing an invitation for spring 1999! This includes Butch *(the Delashaw's son who was a little boy of about three in Walterboro)* and family.

Thanks for helping make a wonderful memory. Please keep in touch.

Love, Lu

The other letter was clearly intended for Ralph Jenkins and his wife, although she did not include a salutation in her notes.

I'm still savoring the momentous time Bruce Anne and I enjoyed with you and Tiero and others. Seeing all of you again brought back so many pleasant memories, memories to be cherished, not forgotten.

I'd like to thank you, Ralph, for making the Parcell clan feel so welcome. Time went so fast and there was so much to say.

Having touched on friendship for the past, I'm very reluctant to let go. I do hope we can keep in touch and visit. I realize Washington is a long way off from N.C. but coming South is what everyone does sooner or later!

Tiero, I've taken a new approach to the piano--maybe even thinking of actually practicing rather than "just playing."

The note ends abruptly here. If there was any further contact, I am unaware of it. We attended no more reunions.

EPILOGUE

Although I am the child of a man who died for his country, I never knew him and did not know enough to appreciate his story, even after meeting some of the men he served with. Then 2014, the year of the seventieth anniversary of D-Day, arrived. On Saturday night, March 1, 2014, about ten o'clock, my phone rang. My immediate thought was, "This cannot be good." No one calls our house at that hour unless they have bad news. But when I answered the call, there was a stranger on the other end. She asked if I were Bruce Anne Shook. Yes, I reluctantly replied, thinking it was kind of late for a call to solicit funds. Then came a second question. "Was your father Bruce Parcell?" Well, yes, again. The stranger then identified herself as Janie Simon from Dallas, Texas. She explained that the town of Picauville in France was planning a big celebration in June to commemorate the D-Day anniversary and they would like for me to come. A monument had been erected to the memory of the pilots who had died while flying out of the A-8 airstrip in the days following the allied invasion. It was to be dedicated on June 5. Janie was trying to locate the children or other surviving family members of those pilots. She was excited that she had found me. At this point I was nearly speechless. I managed to take a deep breath and ask a few questions.

Janie, as it turned out, became involved with World War II veterans and ceremonies honoring them because of her uncle. He had been in the D-Day invasion and had later been a prisoner of war in Germany. Like most veterans, he never talked about his experiences. When he was in his eighties, he went to a Veterans' Hospital and said that he needed help. He was diagnosed with post-traumatic stress disorder, a condition that was not even recognized in the 1940s. Janie took him on an Honor Flight to Washington, D.C., where he laid a wreath at the Tomb of the Unknown Soldier. This helped him so much that Janie decided to begin working with other veterans. This led her to France where she became friends with some of the people who sponsor annual ceremonies in Picauville, the very village where my father had spent the last few weeks of his life.

I talked with Janie for over an hour and told her I would have to discuss the possible trip with my husband. We had just been on a big trip to Central America in January. One of the things we did there was to go to Panama to visit with our old friend Howard Price, whose father had served in the 510th Squadron after my father's death. We also had a trip to Russia planned for July. How in the world could we also go to France in June? But when I explained the situation to my husband David, his first reaction was, "Well, we have to go." We talked and talked, and as a result, we called our travel agent and asked him to help us plan the trip. Within four days we had plane tickets, a rental car, and hotel reservations in Paris, where we planned to stay for four days before we headed out to Normandy.

Meanwhile, I also had to call Janie back and work on the details for our Picauville stay. She put me in touch with Eric Labourdette, who was the vice president of an organization called *Picauville se Souvient*, or *Picauville Remembers*. Eric is from Cherbourg. Because he speaks English, he was the driving force behind the planning of D-Day events in Picauville. We exchanged a few emails, but it was Janie who was our main contact person. She would call frequently to update me on the plans. On June 5 there would be the monument dedication, complete with fly-overs, parachute jumps, and speeches. There was to be a big Friendship Dinner on June 6 which would include French, German, and American soldiers, plus another ceremony to honor the infantrymen who came through Picauville in June of 1944.

All along I was hearing of these plans and thinking, well, we will be there and we will just be part of the audience. It will be interesting. Then Janie reported that General Breedlove was going to make the keynote speech at the monument. Fine, I thought. She also reported that General Jones was coming. Clueless as I was, I had no idea who these men were. But when she told me that General Breedlove had heard my story and would be including it in his speech, I decided it might be prudent to find out about him. Google informed me that Phillip Breedlove was the Supreme Allied Commander of NATO forces in Europe and a four star general. General Noel "Tom" Jones, Vice Commander of NATO Forces in Europe and Africa, was a three star general. This event suddenly took on new significance.

As the weeks went by, Janie had more information for me. Helen Patton, General George Patton's granddaughter, would be in attendance. There would probably be eight hundred people at the Friendship Dinner. I was going to be one of only a few guests of honor. American Airlines had agreed to sponsor the events and would be flying Mary Eisenhower, former President Eisenhower's granddaughter, over for the ceremony. This was getting to be intimidating. I began shopping for some new clothes.

Picauville paratrooper monument, erected in 2002, presumably in reaction to the terrorist bombings in the U.S, September 11, 2001. The pilots' monument is just out of the picture on the left. Wreaths were laid following the ceremonies to commemorate D-Day.

After all the phone calls and emails, we finally arrived in Picauville in our rental car, a brand new Mercedes. With some difficulty we located our little hotel, the Hotel des Voyaugers, which was spartan to say the least. The proprietor spoke no English and we spoke almost no French. She had no reservation for Shook. We were starting to panic when David called me by my nickname, Brucie. "Bruce?" she said. Oui, oui. "Bruce Parcell?" It seemed that, oddly, Eric had made the reservation in my father's name. All was well. I called him to let him know we had arrived and within a few minutes he bounded into the hotel lobby. We were immediately enfolded in bear hugs and initiated into the French practice of kissing both cheeks by way of a greeting. He wanted to take us to the airstrip. He wanted to show us the site of the monument. He wanted us to meet his friend Denis. Enthusiastic does not quite do his demeanor justice. Off

Eric Labourdette and I, sharing a hug. Helen Patton is on the left in the background.

we went in his car to see the sights. Afterwards, he took us to the lovely home of Denis Dennebouy, President of *Picauville se Souvient*. There we watched as the family prepared for the next day by blowing up hundreds of red, white, and blue balloons. Each balloon had a tag with the name of a serviceman who had died there following the invasion. We met Denis's parents, Charles and Nicole. They spoke no English but their hospitality was warm and welcoming. We learned later that Charles had seen his home destroyed by friendly fire during the invasion. He was five years old at the time. Still, he and his whole family feel true affection and gratitude towards Americans, even to this day. The American Airlines dignitaries, including a retired general named Frank Padilla, were also guests at the Denne-

bouys' home, so we met them as well.

Back at the hotel, we met yet another person, Phyllis Kent, who was an Air Force Major stationed in Ramstein, Germany. She was there to help translate the generals' speeches into French. Janie had appointed her to look after us since Janie herself could not travel because of a family illness. Phyllis became our guardian angel and a fast friend. The next morning, June 5, we went with her to the place where the

Phyllis and I on a Picauville street

new monument would be unveiled. A crowd was already gathering when we arrived. There were dozens of vintage World War II military vehicles in the parking area, driven by French re-enactors. It was amazing sight.

French re-enactors in Picauville at the site of the monuments to the paratroopers and pilots.

Another scene with French re-enactors

Finally, after much milling around and some delays, the ceremony began. David and I were given seats of honor on the second row, just behind the military brass. Here is an excerpt from General Breedlove's speech:

> Brucie grew up never knowing her father, only the tales of his bravery and his heroic actions from those who served with him. Brucie's life was irrevocably changed that night, and it is impossible for us to understand the personal price she has paid over her lifetime, for the freedom of strangers. Brucie, your father's actions have made those strangers,…and their families,…your friends forever. I can feel their love for you today, and I can feel their love for all the family members of the men who fought in this area. Thank you for being here.

General Phillip Breedlove, Supreme Allied Commander of NATO Forces in Europe

Following General Breedlove, General Padilla was introduced so that he might read a letter from Ralph Jenkins, the man who had succeeded my father as commander of the 510th Fighter Squadron. After some comments and the reading of the letter, General Padilla announced that I wanted to say a few words. This was a complete surprise to me, but what was I to do? I made my way to the podium for a very short speech in which I ex-

General Frank Padilla, retired from the Air Force and now with American Airlines

pressed my gratitude to the people of Picauville for inviting me there and for honoring the memory of my father. Merci. Then I sat back down quickly. After it was all over, many people came up to me to say "Thank you," for my sacrifice. Some had tears in their eyes. Later, I commented to Phyllis that all I had done was to get born. Still, it was a wonderful outpouring of love and gratitude.

Label with my father's name on it attached to a balloon. Amazingly, a woman I met later at the Dennebouys' home had randomly snapped this picture. She pulled out her phone to show me, only to realize that out of all the balloons she could have chosen, she had picked the one with my father's name.

On D-Day itself, we made it a point to stay away from the beaches where the major events of the day were taking place. Many heads of state including President Obama, Queen Elizabeth, and Russian President Vladimir Putin were on hand to commemorate the invasion. Access was very limited, security was tight, and traffic was terrible. We had the day to ourselves and used it to explore the inland area, including a visit to a cemetery in the small village of Orglandes where thousands of German soldiers are buried. Then it was time for the second ceremony in Picauville, held at the site of the monument to the infantrymen who helped to liberate the town. General Jones was the keynote speaker there. Unexpectedly, he also made my father the centerpiece of his speech. Here, in part, are his comments:

General Noel "Tom" Jones, Vice Commander of NATO Forces in Europe and Africa. Beside him are Picauville's mayor; Denis Dennebouy, the president of Picauville se Souvient; and Eric.

On D-Day Bruce was the air commander, leading his pilots to perform close air support for ground troops. Over the next few weeks, Bruce flew with tenacity, leading his squadron to take out heavily defended German targets. His squadron was forward deployed to Site A8, known by the Aviation Engineering Battalions as "Picauville." On 27 July Bruce was performing a strafing mission on enemy targets when he was hit by enemy fire and could not bail out,…he died in the ensuing crash. In a letter written to Bruce's wife Lu, Parcell was described as a "true hero,…with a patriotic spirit,…courageous heart,…and a determined will." Brucie is here with us tonight to honor the memory of the father she never met. Bruce Parcell was one of approximately two thousand men lost during the invasion of France…Although Bruce died for freedom at a young age, he left a legacy of freedom honored forever by his daughter,…grandchildren, great-grandchildren and the people of Picauville.

After that it was time for dinner. We made our way, along with hundreds of others, to the local school gymnasium where there were more speeches. The other guests of honor and I were made honorary members of *Picauville se Souvient*. Because of the size of the crowd, dinner was not served until about ten o'clock. It had been a long, emotionally draining day, so after nibbling on overcooked steak and cool French fries, we called it a night and went back to the hotel, in need of a good night's sleep.

The Friendship Dinner, with over 800 in attendance. Phyllis and I are in the left hand front corner.

The following day, all that was left was to say good-bye to our new-found friends. Eric came by and took us again to the Dennebouys where we were introduced to a room full of Americans and French people. Few of us spoke both languages, so it was an interesting experience. But once again we felt the love that the French people in Normandy have for Americans. Eric told us that his mother, grandmother, and aunt had lived for four years with German soldiers occupying their home. Denis showed us his enormous collection of World War II memorabilia, including helmets with bullet holes in them, first aid supplies, uniforms, weapons of all sorts, even a gas mask for a horse. A man named Dominique read aloud for me the section of Remy Chuinard's book that describes my father's crash. He had to translate it from the French as he went along and became concerned for my feelings as he realized how graphic the description was. The war is still very much with these people and they have not forgotten the sacrifice that so many made to liberate them from an occupying enemy.

As for me, I came home with a new appreciation for my father's role in the war. The fairy tale that was my parents' romance and marriage came to a tragic end far too soon. However, I am very grateful for the letters that both of them saved. They lay in a blanket chest at the foot of Mother's bed until her death in 2008. No one in the family knew what a treasure that chest contained. She did not choose to share the letters while she was alive, but I like to think that she would be glad for their seeing the light of day now. The telling of their story has helped me finally to understand a portion of my parents' lives that I would otherwise never have known. And as I said in the beginning, "What a story it is!"

Picauville monument to the pilots who died flying out of the A-8 airstrip in the days following D-Day.

Poster that advertised D-Day activities in Picauville in 2014. Bruce's picture is in the v-point of the collage of black and white photos.

Monument at the American Cemetery, Colville sur Mer.

Grave at the American Cemetery near Colville sur Mer, Normandy, overlooking Omaha Beach

BIBLIOGRAPHIC NOTES

I have drawn upon several sources in compiling this book of letters. First and foremost after my parents' letters are my own memories from childhood and the scant stories told to me by my mother and grandmother. There are also many letters, not included here, from my mother to her parents during the time that she was in college. Piecing all of that information together, along with the story that revealed itself in the letters themselves, was like putting together a jigsaw puzzle without the picture of the puzzle on the box. Old photographs that I have looked at all my life suddenly began to make sense in light of the things I was learning. For example, there is a close-up picture of Mother as a young woman sitting in the driver's seat of a car. By comparing it with a labeled picture of her and my father that was taken the day that they parted for the last time, I know now that she was getting ready to get in that car, a green Buick, and drive from Walterboro, South Carolina, to Barium Springs. I also know that this was the last time my father saw her before he died.

In my family archives there are a number of yellowed newspaper clippings from the war years. None of them are dated and almost none indicate which newspaper they came from. I had to infer this from the contents of the letters.

Mother and I lived at Barium Springs with my grandparents from the time of my birth until she remarried in 1950. I have many fond memories of the people and places there. To fill in the history, I used *An Album of Memories: the Presbyterian Orphans' Home at Barium Springs, North Carolina* by Charles M. Barrett, Editor, 1994.

For the information on my father's various medals, I relied on Wikipedia, looking up the Air Medal, Oak Leaf Clusters, and Distinguished Flying Cross at en.m.wikipedia.org. Wikipedia also enabled me to learn about the movie *I Wanted Wings* and about the *Mauretania*.

The information on Camp Shanks was entirely new to me. I used a website at don.genmcguire.com that contained an article entitled "Camp Shanks, New York." *The Hudson River Valley* magazine at hvmag.com published an article, "Remembering Camp Shanks," by David Levine, on August 16, 2010, that was helpful. At hudsonrivervalley.com, I found information on Camp Shanks World War II Museum.

Jenkins Jerry Junkers: The World War II 510th Fighter Squadron is a book compiled by Ralph Jenkins and Charles Mohrle for one of the squadron reunions. I discovered it in my mother's belonging after her death. It provided much valuable information.

Ralph Jenkins was quoted extensively in a "Dedication" on the website 510fs. org. The date was May 3, 2012. There he reminisced about Walterboro, Camp Shanks, the *Mauretania* ocean crossing, Christchurch, bombing tactics, D-Day, and Picauville. Ralph was also quoted in an article from February 23, 1990, called "From P47 Thunderbolt to A-10 Thunderbolt 11" by Barbara Buzette. This appeared in a publication called *The Forum*.

Another book that was extremely helpful in filling in the blanks about military activities of the 510th squadron was *Thunder Monsters over Europe: A History of the 405th Fighter Group in World War II* by Reginald G. Nolte, Sunflower University Press, Manhattan, Kansas, 1986. Mother acquired this book when we attended a fighter group reunion.

The French author Remy Chuinard wrote *Stormy Sky over Normandy*, translated from the French by Emmanuel Pierreuse, copyright 2000. Pages 116-118 from the English translation are referenced.

ACKNOWLEDGEMENTS

This book was born on the night that Janie Simon called to invite me to Picauville for the seventieth anniversary of D-Day. If not for her persistence in searching for me, my parents' letters might still be sitting in shoeboxes in my attic. Janie has a particular calling to help connect World War II veterans and their families with their history. She has told me that if I had been named anything other than Bruce, she probably never would have found me. I will always be grateful to her for her successful search and her late night phone call.

The next stage in this saga came when my husband and I returned from our trip to Picauville. We almost immediately drove to Ocracoke Island, North Carolina, for a storytelling workshop led by Donald Davis, storyteller extraordinaire. This was not our first workshop experience with Donald, so I knew that I could develop the story of our trip and our Normandy experiences in a welcoming environment. Donald creates a safe and nurturing space for novice and veteran storytellers alike. It was on Ocracoke that I first told the "end of the story," along with a little background about my parents and their relationship. I did not know then how much I didn't know, but I was about to find out.

Upon returning home after the workshop, Jeri Rowe came to my house to interview me. He was at that time a feature writer for the Greensboro *News and Record.* Jeri and I talked for about two hours. At the end of our time together, he became excited when I told him I had photos, letters, and telegrams. The result of all this was an illustrated newspaper article detailing my story. It appeared in the *News and Record* on Sunday, July 6, 2014. It was, I thought, a terrific article. I heard from many friends and relatives who thought so also. I decided that maybe my story would be of interest to people outside my immediate circle of friends. For the first time, I realized what a treasure trove of memories my mother had left me.

Sometime later, I discovered that a friend in my YMCA exercise class had written a book. It was based on love letters exchanged between her Quaker grandparents when they were courting in the 1920s. Ann Trueblood Raper's book, *A Quaker Courtship,* was another source of inspiration for me. It is a lovely book and a wonderful tribute to her grandparents. I began to think that maybe I too could write a book.

By the time I met Ann, I had already transcribed my parents' letters. The process of first arranging, and then painstakingly typing the letters, was very hard. I spent many days at my keyboard with tears running down my cheeks.

I finally understood just what my parents meant to each other, and what they had been through during the time of their relationship. Once I finished, these letters were sitting there on my computer in a giant file called "Letters, Bruce and Frances." It was time to do something with them.

The book finally began to come together with the encouragement of my husband David. What had begun as a project that I was working on alone became one of teamwork. He carefully read each letter and made corrections of typographical errors. He examined postmarks under a magnifying glass to piece together just when each one had been written. As the book took shape, we realized that we had many old family pictures that would make the story more real. David spent hundreds of hours with our scanner and Photoshop, editing and cleaning up those old photographs, many of which were much the worse for wear. He scanned objects such as the Distinguished Flying Cross and my father's Air Corps wings and made them look fantastic as images. He also offered invaluable advice on some of the wording of the text, not to mention endless proofreading. I didn't always agree with his advice, so this was not always an entirely smooth journey. What you have just read has my name on it as the author, but he had a big hand in making this book what it is. For that I am extremely grateful.

Finally, I would like to thank Melissa Blackburn, book designer, who took an extremely rough draft and made it into something that I am very proud of. She also showed extraordinary patience with all the changes that we kept making to the book for days on end.

This entire project has been a labor of love. I hope you, the reader, have come away richer for having learned of my story. Thanks for letting me share it.

A FEW MORE MEMORIES

All the Parcell girls at a Fraley family reunion, 1984. Left to right: Sarah, Nancy, Blanche, Brucie, Katherine.

Frances, Brucie, and Anne Winslow on a family beach trip to Pawley's Island, S.C., sometime in the 1990s.

Brucie, sister Rowena, and brother Chris with Frances on Thanksgiving, 2007, just months before Frances's death. The whole family came together for a joyous celebration.

Left to right: newly promoted Lt. Col. Phyllis Kent, Janie Simon, and Brucie enjoying dinner near Washington, D.C., in November, 2016.

Brucie's family in 2016. Far left: Daughter Amy and her husband Art Swanson, granddaughters Sydney and Natalie; center: son Alex with granddaughter Ellen and wife Brooke Smith; rear right: husband David and Brucie.

Amy, David, Brucie, and Alex at the American Cemetery on June 10, 2017, Bruce's one hundredth birthday.

Eric Labourdette and Brucie, June 10 2017.

Missing Man Formation
An aerial salute to a fallen pilot

Made in the USA
Lexington, KY
15 September 2017